GERMANY AND IRELAND
1945–1955

Germany and Ireland
1945–1955
Two Nations' Friendship

CATHY MOLOHAN

IRISH ACADEMIC PRESS
DUBLIN • PORTLAND, OR

First published in 1999 by
IRISH ACADEMIC PRESS
44, Northumberland Road, Dublin 4, Ireland
and in the United States of America by
IRISH ACADEMIC PRESS
c/o ISBS, 5804 NE Hassalo Street,
Portland, OR 97213 3644

Website: www.iap.ie

British Library Cataloguing in Publication Data
Molohan, Cathy
  Germany and Ireland, 1945–1955 : two nations' friendship
  1. Ireland – Foreign relations – Germany   2. Germany – Foreign relations –
Ireland   3. Ireland – Politics and government – 1949–   4. Germany – Social
Conditions
  I. Title
  327.4'15'043

  ISBN 0–7165–2631–X hardback
  ISBN 0–7165–2708–1 paperback

Library of Congress Cataloguing-in-Publication Data
Molohan, Cathy, 1972–
  Germany and Ireland, 1945–1955 : two nations' friendship / Cathy
Molohan.
     p.   cm.
  Includes bibliographical references (p.   ) and index.
  ISBN 0–7165–2631–X hardback
  ISBN 0–7165–2708–1 paperback
  1. Ireland—Foreign relations—Germany. 2. Germany—Foreign relations—
Ireland. 3. Ireland—Foreign relations—1922– 4. Germany—Foreign
relations—1945– I. Title.
  DA964.G3M65   1999
  327.415043—DC21   99–13449
                                                      CIP

Typeset in 11 pt on 13 pt Sabon by
Carrigboy Typesetting Services, County Cork
Printed by Creative Print & Design (Wales), Ebbw Vale

Contents

ILLUSTRATIONS

Acknowledgements

M y special thanks go to my supervisor, Professor Dr B. J. Wendt, whose support and suggestions at the University of Hamburg during my exchange year in 1992–93 and during my research work were invaluable. I also thank Dr Axel Schildt for his supervision. Many thanks to Dr Alan Kramer, Director of European Studies at Trinity College, Dublin, who inspired me to take up this research through his support and encouragement during my time at Trinity.

I greatly appreciate the help of Ernest Berkenheier, Helmut and Elisabeth Clissmann, Michael Donnellan, Sean Egan, J. B. Gubbins, Peter Kaudewitz, Rosemary Kavanagh, Joe McQuillean, Joe Roche, Dermot Tittle, and especially Enno Stephan, Eberhard Langer and Herbert Remmel, without whose personal memories of the period this book would not have been complete.

I would like to thank the staff of the National Archives, Dublin, the Institut für Internationale Angelegenheiten in Hamburg, the Hamburger Weltwirtschaftsarchiv, the Public Records Office, London, Martin Good of the Red Cross in Dublin, Wolfgang Strecker of the Deutscher Caritasverband Freiburg, the Politisches Archiv des Auswärtigen Amtes in Bonn, in particular Dr Frhr von Boeselager, Dr Schmidt-Supprian and Arne Schneider of the Goethe Institut Dublin, and Mr Meyer-Wiefhausen and Mario Haas of the German Embassy in Dublin.

The German Academic Exchange Service (DAAD) assisted me in carrying out my research through a scholarship, for which I am very grateful.

Katharina Jakob proof-read the German version of this book and I owe her my thanks for her hard work.

Finally I would like to thank my parents and my family. Without their love and support, both emotional and financial, during my years of study, this project would not have been possible.

Introduction

German–Irish relations are based on centuries-old contacts between the two countries, the best known of which were for a long time cultural, religious and military. Today when Germans think of Ireland, the majority has a picture of the Emerald Isle with red-haired, romantic people and traditional pubs. In Ireland, Germany is the land of the economic miracle, hard-working people and also, for some, a former enemy of Britain's. There is, however, another chapter of German–Irish relations, one which has not yet been documented in its entirety. These are the relations in the decade after the Second World War – a decade of soldiers and spies, humanitarian aid, dissent between the Irish government and the Allied powers on German issues, and also the decade in which both countries were declared republics. It is a period in which German–Irish relations changed considerably. Up to the beginning of the twentieth century, the emphasis of the relations had been cultural and religious. These connections are characterised, to name some of the most important events, by the large number of Irish monks in German territories from the seventh century on; the four thousand Lutheran refugees who fled to Ireland in the eighteenth century, and by the dedicated research in Celtic Studies in Germany carried out by academics such as Rudolf Thurneysen in the early twentieth century.

It was in the early 1900s that national aspirations entered into German–Irish relations and changed their character from connections based on religious and academic life to those of a political nature. The most important of these were the existence of a small German–Irish society in Berlin which supported the cause of Irish independence, the military assistance given by Germany to Ireland in 1916 and the German attempts to support the IRA against Britain and to use Ireland as an information base during the Second World War.

It is intended in this book to examine German–Irish relations from 1945 to 1955 in view of these aforementioned established relations, and also the newer aspects. Where possible, both sides will be dealt

1

with, i.e. the connections in Ireland with Germany and vice-versa. In order to simplify the expression, the phrase 'German–Irish relations' was chosen to portray both sides. In many cases, the contacts between both countries were not on an equal basis; the Irish put far more emphasis on relations with Germany than did Germany on Irish relations, particularly in the political field. The significance of this difference in perception will be explored in itself. In the first two chapters, Irish relations with Great Britain and America as Allied powers are also of importance when discussing German–Irish relations.

The book concentrates on six main areas. These are:

- the state of German–Irish relations before the war;
- the effect of the Second World War on the links between the two countries;
- the resumption of diplomatic, economic and cultural relations in the 1950s, each of these containing important European elements;
- the political relations between the two countries, in particular from the point of view of the value Ireland placed on the division of both countries as a common issue.

One topic which arises in every chapter, and which represents one of the basic theses of this study, is the role that politics played in German–Irish relations. It will be seen that Germany was important for Irish politicians in two ways in the 1940s and 1950s: firstly, Germany was used after the war to distinguish Ireland's position from that of Great Britain, in that Irish politicians dealt with German citizens in Ireland as they saw fit and thereby provoked strong criticism from the Allies; secondly, from 1949 onwards the Federal Republic of Germany was seen as a main target of Irish propaganda against the partition of the country, since both Germany and Ireland shared a common fate regarding the division of their national territories. Irish politicians hoped that Germany and Ireland could work together against these divisions.

Although Ireland was neutral in the Second World War, the war did have a considerable effect on the country. The first part of this study will concentrate on the results of the problems that were created for Ireland by the internment and imprisonment of German soldiers and spies in the country. This was an issue of contention which led to considerable strain on Irish–American and especially on Irish–British relations. De Valera, who was Taoiseach for most of this period, used the demands made by the Allies that Ireland should deport German citizens in order to prove Irish independence from Great Britain by not yielding to Allied pressure in the matter. German soldiers and spies were allowed to remain in Ireland until de Valera could be sure that they would be treated fairly in Germany, and that he had proved his point to the British authorities. In regard to diplomacy, the question of the German diplomatic staff who had remained in Ireland during the war had to be dealt with by the Irish government after 1945. Politics featured here again, with de Valera granting the men residence permits instead of handing them over to the Allies, as had been demanded.

The topic of the fourth chapter is the humanitarian assistance which Ireland gave Germany after the war. Aid from Ireland was given more quickly and was proportionally speaking more generous than that from all other European states. A large part of this contribution to the relief of Germany was made by one organisation – the Save the German Children Society – which made it possible for hundreds of German children to be fostered in Ireland from 1946–1949. Politics also played a role in this area. It must be asked to what extent Germany's position as a former enemy of England featured as a motive in Irish help for Germany.

The relations resumed between the two countries after the war in the fields of diplomacy, the economy and culture. There are close links between the topics of diplomacy and trade, since the tasks of Irish diplomats after 1950 were largely developing economic contacts between the two countries. Economic relations with Germany were particularly important for Ireland for two reasons: Germany could provide Ireland with machines and technology which were not available in Ireland, and Ireland could hope to reduce her economic dependence on Great Britain while strengthening continental ties.

Cultural relations are the longest existing relations between Ireland and Germany. During, and immediately after, the war such contacts were mostly impossible. There was one man in this time, Heinrich Becker, who tried to maintain German–Irish cultural contacts. His political record was not, however, without blemish, as will be seen. From 1947 onwards the contacts flourished again with the support of both countries. These relations were mostly based on a small circle of dedicated academics, authors and interested citizens. The German–Irish and Irish–German societies that were founded in several places in both countries after the war were of particular importance in promoting cultural relations between the two peoples. Such matters were also of interest to the Irish government politically, and again were in part used as a means to disseminate knowledge in Germany about the political situation in Ireland.

Finally, political relations will be covered in this book, with special emphasis on the division of Ireland and Germany and the significance of propaganda in this issue. In particular, the importance of writers and journalists in disseminating political propaganda will be examined. Because of the fact that the press played an important role in forming public opinion about each respective country, the Irish and German press will be analysed in detail. The emphasis which Ireland placed on Germany as a target of Irish propaganda will be pointed out, while it will be shown that German interest in Ireland tended to be based more on a cultural and tourist level.

There is a considerable amount of literature available on German–Irish relations before and during the second World War; only a small amount, however, on relations after the war. Enno Stephan's *Spies in Ireland* or T. Ryle Dwyer's *Guests of the State* are excellent works on specific aspects of post-war relations, but no book has been published which examines the entirety of these relations.

This study is based mainly on primary sources, most of which are to be found in the national archives in Dublin, Bonn and London, as well as on newspaper analysis and interviews with contemporaries. In the National Archives, Dublin, the files of the Department of Foreign Affairs (DFA) were examined. These files contain a considerable amount of information and contributed most to this study.

In Bonn, the files of the departments I–IV of the political archives of the Department of Foreign Affairs (Auswärtiges Amt) were also very important. A large amount of the information in this study is taken from the reports of Katzenberger, the German envoy in Dublin to the German Department of Foreign Affairs (which are to be found in departments II and III). Also available here are various newspaper clippings on the topic of German–Irish relations. Department IV contains information on the cultural relations between the two countries.

In the Public Records Office in London, the files of the Foreign Office (FO) and the Dominions Office (DO) were examined. These files contain a wealth of information about the time directly after the war, for example about the fate of German internees and spies, the issue of the German diplomats in Ireland, and about the Save the German Children Society, which, together with the files from the National Archives in Dublin, were able to provide a complete picture of this period.

The Institute of International Affairs in Hamburg and the Hamburg World Trade Archive (Weltwirtschafts Archiv) were particularly useful in providing newspaper clippings.

The files of the Irish Red Cross in Dublin were made available to me for this study. These mainly contain information about humanitarian aid for Germany after the war and especially about co-operation with the Save the German Children Society.

The Catholic Caritas Association in Freiburg also provided me with information concerning the Irish aid for Germany and, in particular, the assistance given to the town of Freiburg.

A complete picture of this period would never have been possible without the help of those involved at the time. Enno Stephan told me about the question of the German spies in Ireland and the fate of the German children who came to Ireland after the war. Helmut and Elisabeth Clissmann also gave me a lot of information on these two topics. Various people who were involved in the Save the German Children Society at the time told me about their personal involvement (see bibliography).

CHAPTER ONE

The pre-war period

TRADE AND DIPLOMACY BEFORE THE WAR

After the foundation of the Irish Free State (Saorstát) in 1922, Irish politicians set about the task of developing through actions the independence from Britain that they had not fully achieved on paper. The desire to establish freedom from Britain in every walk of life was evident. Economically, the Irish currency was linked to Sterling and Irish banking was dependent on the Bank of England. The extent of the dependence on Britain became evident during the trade war which lasted from 1932 to 1938. However, the 1930s were also a time in which links with other trading nations took on increasing importance, psychologically in terms of perceived greater independence, as well as economically. The trade relations between Germany and Ireland before the Second World War were of some importance, although Ireland placed more emphasis on encouraging these than did Germany. The conditions for trade between Germany and Ireland had been established in an agreement in 1930 and were based mainly on the export of agricultural products to Germany and the import of machines to Ireland[1]. In 1935 a further agreement was signed in which Irish exports to Germany in relation to imports from that country were fixed at a ratio of 1:3. In 1936 a ratio of 1:2 was agreed upon. The trade deficit which is apparent here remained in place up to the war and the situation did not change to Ireland's advantage in the 1950s.

Irish foreign policy in the 1920s and 1930s was also hallmarked by the aim of achieving the widest possible recognition of the rights of the country as a free nation. The 1920s saw a time of active construction in Irish foreign relations. In 1923 Ireland became a member of the League of Nations and was the first of the Commonwealth countries to establish a permanent delegation in Geneva. In the following years, Irish representatives were accredited in London and Washington and trade attachés in Paris and Brussels.

In 1928, Joseph Walshe, Secretary of the Department of External Affairs, introduced changes which led to more widespread international representation. One of the results of this drive was that a legation was opened in Berlin in 1929. It was led by Daniel Binchy, a lawyer and authority on Germany and its history. Binchy's main aim was to improve the economic relations between Ireland and Germany. Alongside gaining recognition for Ireland's political position, economic interests were to be of prime importance for Irish envoys in Germany in the 1930s and again in the 1950s. The fact that a trade agreement was drawn up as soon as 1930 illustrates the priority that trade issues had in the burgeoning inter-state relations.

In 1933, when Binchy left the service, he was replaced by Charles Bewley. This was an unfortunate choice for Irish diplomatic relations with Germany, since Bewley drew more and more attention to himself as time progressed through his flippant, pro-National Socialist behaviour. He was withdrawn from his post as a result of this in 1939. It turned out to be impossible to have a replacement named, since Irish diplomats still had to be accredited by the English King and this was impossible given the international climate. Bewley's secretary, William Warnock, carried out his duties in the legation during the war until the building was destroyed by a bomb in 1944. John Duggan described Warnock thus: 'In his quiet way he complemented Hempel's work [see below] in Dublin in keeping Irish–German relations on an even keel during an extraordinarily difficult period.'[2]

The first German envoy to Ireland, Georg von Dehn-Schmidt, was named in 1930. In 1937 he was replaced by Dr Eduard Hempel, and it was the latter who represented Germany in Ireland during the war.

The result of this combined diplomatic and economic effort was that by 1938 Germany was Ireland's fourth largest source of imports – after Britain, Belgium and the USA – and Germany had become the second largest export market for Irish products after Britain (part of the reason for this being the trade war with Britain). Ireland exported mainly cattle, horses, agricultural products and wool to Germany, and imported machines, electrical goods, iron and steel products and fertilisers. Individual contacts between German and Irish companies remained at a low level throughout this period, however, a fact which was to change slowly after 1945. In the meantime, it was the turn of the secret service and the Department of External Affairs to take over in German–Irish relations in the war years to come.

THE MILITARY BACKGROUND – THE FIRST WORLD WAR

German military interest in Ireland's fate did not begin with the outbreak of the Second World War. The long Irish fight for independence from Britain, which erupted again in 1916, had not been ignored in Germany, and the Irish rebels knew that Germany could turn out to be a useful source of assistance. The story of Roger Casement is the best known of the incidents that occurred involving Germany during the First World War. Casement travelled to Germany in 1916 to accomplish two things – firstly, to form an Irish brigade from the Irish internees in Germany[3] and secondly, to organise German weapons for Ireland. He was informed that the Germans could not send any men to Ireland, but that there was the possibility of sending weapons.[4] The plans were discovered by the British, however, and the ship with the weapons was stopped. Roger Casement was hanged on 3 August, 1916.

In 1918, as the Irish conflict with Britain grew increasingly critical, an Irish prisoner of war in Germany, Joseph Dowling, was sent to Ireland by the Germans in order to make contact with Sinn Féin.[5] He was arrested immediately. Such incidents did not further the Irish cause against the British; indeed the Dowling case was used by Britain as an excuse to arrest leading Sinn Féin members, since it claimed that Dowling was part of a German conspiracy in Ireland.

These plots, although they failed, indicated a willingness on the part of some German military leaders to help the Irish cause if they thought that they could damage Britain in doing this. In the Second World War plans existed to send Irishmen who had been trained in sabotage in Germany to Ireland in order to assist the IRA in its bombing campaign on the British mainland, launched in January 1939. These plans resulted chiefly in two episodes. Firstly, in 1940 there was an attempt to form an Irish brigade from Irishmen who had been taken prisoner in their capacity as part of the British Army. Although ten men were chosen for this project, the plan was dropped in the end for unknown reasons but probably due to the fact that by then Hitler had turned his attention to the Eastern Front. Secondly, the Germans attempted to send two IRA members who were in Germany at the time to Ireland to cause political trouble for the government. These were Seán Russell, an IRA leader who had been in America at the outbreak of war and who had been brought to Germany, and Frank Ryan, who had been a prisoner of war in Spain before 'fleeing' with the help of the Germans. Russell died in August 1940 on board a submarine which was to bring the men to Ireland. Ryan then returned to Germany where he died in 1944.[6] These events did not have any effect on German–Irish relations after 1945 and so will not be dealt with in any further detail. The scheme which had the biggest impact on Ireland and Irish–Allied relations after the war was the attempt in 1940–1941 to place German spies in Ireland.

CHAPTER TWO

Soldiers, spies and diplomats

IRELAND IN THE EMERGENCY

The presence of German diplomatic staff, captured spies and interned soldiers in Ireland was a severe strain on Irish–Allied relations in 1945. Contention between Ireland and the Allies regarding German citizens in Ireland had already arisen earlier in the war, especially in regard to the German diplomatic staff. Despite hefty protests by the British and especially the American representative in Ireland, Dr Hempel and his legation staff were still carrying out their duties in Ireland in the spring of 1945. The British press described the German envoy and his staff as spies who had considerably damaged the Allied cause through their reports to Berlin. Articles in the American and British press after the war spread the rumour that the Irish government had secretly done all it could to help the Germans and had thus damaged the Allied war effort. This point of view was widely accepted by the British public:

> Commonly, residents in Allied countries believed that Ireland crawled with spies, that German sub[marine]s refuelled off the Irish coast with help from Irish dissidents, that Eamon de Valera – who served both as Prime Minister and Minister of External Affairs throughout the war – would do anything to hurt Britain, and that if Ireland had permitted the British to use her ports the Allied war effort would have been greatly facilitated.[1]

This opinion could not be supported by facts. While de Valera had always behaved in a neutral fashion outwardly, he had occasionally closed an eye to certain events – not to help the Germans, but to support the Allies: 'Despite an outward appearance of rigidity, Irish neutrality was applied ultimately in a very indulgent manner towards the Allies.'[2]

An example of this is the policy of the Irish government regarding English and American soldiers on the one hand, and German soldiers on the other. If English or American pilots or sailors were forced to land in Ireland by technical problems, or did so accidentally, they were often permitted to leave the country or to 'escape'. German soldiers, however, were almost always detained for the duration. De Valera also allowed Allied aeroplanes to fly in Irish airspace, and he did not pass any law forbidding Irish citizens to join a foreign army, as many other neutral countries did, with the result that between 150,000 and 180,000 Irishmen joined the British army.[3]

Hempel himself constantly tried to ensure that Irish neutrality would not be impinged upon by warning his superiors against taking any steps against Ireland. He did not want spies to be sent to Ireland or contact to be made with the IRA. Spies *were* sent, and a plan did exist on paper for the invasion of Ireland, but Hempel was never party to such schemes. Nothing of any consequence was undertaken by the German legation which could have damaged Ireland's neutrality or helped Germany in the war. Indeed, the only transmitter which the legation possessed had been seized in 1943 so that no secret messages could be sent to Germany. Alongside the fact that Hempel was not interested in causing problems for Ireland, the legation was so closely watched by the Irish Secret Service that Hempel could not have done anything of significance even if he had wanted to. Another contributory factor to Hempel's respect for Irish neutrality was that his relations with de Valera were on a friendly basis. All in all, it can be said that Hempel behaved impeccably towards the Irish government during the war and enjoyed de Valera's respect much more than did David Gray, the American representative. Only one member of the German legation staff, Henning Thomsen, drew attention to himself by behaving suspiciously. He got involved in 'cultural' affairs by giving lectures to the Gaelic League which were not only cultural but also political in nature.[4] He was known to sympathise with the Nazis and celebrated German victories openly. Enno Stephan has also expressed the suspicion that Thomsen was involved with the Blueshirts.[5] Hempel was not involved in any of this, however, and Thomsen alone could not bring about much except that he was even more strictly observed by the Irish secret service than were the other members of staff.

While the majority of the Irish people supported the Allied war cause, there were a number of individuals who were fanatically pro-German. It was well known in Secret Service and Garda circles that an organisation called the Cumann Naisiunta, whose professed aim was to further the Irish language and culture, was in fact being used as a cover for an organisation calling itself Irish Friends of Germany: 'The Society Cumann Naisiunta is ostensibly for the purpose of promoting the Irish language but is obviously intended as a cover for propaganda, letters etc.'[6] This organisation was active in 1940, and was extremely pro-National Socialist, anti-British and anti-Semitic. Of one of its main members, Maurice O'Connor, a Garda report stated: 'He is obsessed with National Socialist and Corporate Party ideas and aspirations.'[7] The membership of the Irish Friends of Germany and Cumann Naisiunta was numerically insignificant, most of the meetings being attended by less than ten people. Attempts were made to distribute propaganda leaflets in Dublin and around the country, however, and the tone of these borrowed heavily from National Socialist propaganda. In one, entitled *The Jewish Question must be faced*, the existence of a worldwide Jewish plot was claimed:

> Failure to solve the Jewish problem in the past has caused two subversive movements to come into being, viz. Bolshevism and Zionism. The first seeks to destroy Gentile society, the second to establish a Jewish super-government upon the ruins.[8]

In another, *Guth na Firinne*, the Irish people were urged to support their 'true Allies', the Germans, who had supported the Irish culture while Britain was suppressing the country. An effort was also made to recruit army personnel into the organisation. It emerged that three soldiers had been present at a meeting on 4 September, 1940 at which one of them stated that 'a lot of the soldiers would prefer fighting against the government than against Hitler.'[9] The soldiers in question were interrogated and disciplined, and their attitude cannot be said to be representative of that of the Irish army. However, the fact that such an organisation existed illustrates the hope cherished by some that, once again, England's difficulty would be used as Ireland's opportunity.

While being politically and morally reprehensible, incidents such as those described above did not represent a serious threat to Ireland's safety. Nevertheless, despite the country's neutrality and Hempel's desire to have this respected, and the vigilance of G2, there were moments of danger for Ireland when it was feared that the threat of war on the island was coming closer. In 1940 particularly, rumours were rampant that a German invasion or a preventative English occupation were looming. In this atmosphere of fear, stories of

Germans caught in Ireland, dressed in overcoats and carrying radios and maps, fuelled the belief that the 'Third Reich' was indeed planning an attack on Ireland. The vigilance of the Irish population, which resulted in any suspicious foreigner being reported immediately, and the effective work of the Secret Service led to quick arrests of German spies in most cases. The failure of the Germans in their attempt to conquer England led to an abatement of the danger for Ireland. In 1945, however, the issue of those spies who were being held in Irish prisons was brought up by the Allies, who demanded their immediate deportation. The ensuing discord between Ireland and the Allies was one of the major issues to be dealt with by the Irish government immediately after the war.

The spies were not the only Germans in Irish hands at this time. There was also a considerable number of soldiers who had been interned in Ireland for the duration. Their fate was also of interest to the Allies and again the Irish government differed with the former regarding their treatment. The question of those German internees and spies who were in Ireland in 1945 is one of the most interesting and most complex of German–Irish post-war relations. It can be said that the topic overshadowed Irish–American and Irish–British relations and, at the same, time contributed to a positive image of Ireland in Germany. As the war drew to a close, the Allies made it increasingly clear that the presence of German citizens in Ireland was seen as an intolerable situation by them. De Valera, however, was determined to treat the diplomats, soldiers and spies as *he* saw fit and not as the Allies wished. The question of the internees, i.e. those German soldiers whose planes had crashed or who had been ship-wrecked off Ireland, and that of the spies, who had been imprisoned for the crime of entering Ireland illegally with the intention of causing harm to the state, must be dealt with separately due to the different significance of the two groups and their varying treatment.

THE CURRAGH INTERNMENT CAMP

By the end of the war in May 1945, there were 261 German internees in Ireland. Of these, 209 were from the Navy and 52 from the Luftwaffe.[10] The majority – 164 – were survivors of a naval battle in the Bay of Biscay who had been rescued by an Irish freight ship, the *Kerlogue*, in dramatic conditions in December 1943. The men were kept in the Curragh camp in Co. Kildare where the conditions of imprisonment were not particularly harsh. Dr Hempel became involved in the care of the internees, doing his best to reconcile them to their detainment in Ireland. He visited the men rescued by the *Kerlogue* shortly after their arrival in the Curragh in order to raise their spirits.[11] He did his best to ensure that the soldiers had sufficient distraction so that they would not become too restless. Due to his efforts, eighteen of the internees were actually allowed to study in University College Dublin; they were financed by the German legation which collected money from Germans living in Ireland for this purpose. Those men who remained in camp also enjoyed relaxed conditions with a considerable amount of freedom. Dr Hempel received money for the soldiers from Germany which served as pocket-money, while the Irish government was responsible for their upkeep. Many activities took place in the camp including English and meteorology lessons, football, volleyball and music. The men could leave the camp on parole until midnight, and sometimes for longer on special occasions to go to pubs, dances and horse races.[12] They became a familiar and, especially in the case of the young ladies, welcome sight to the people of Kildare. Social events inevitably led to romances with local girls, and some of these developed into serious relationships, strengthening the bond to Ireland for many of the soldiers.

From 1944, however, the prisoners had to cope with financial difficulties since the German government, fighting an increasingly futile battle, sent less and less money. Dr Hempel asked the Irish Red Cross for help, but was refused by the committee: 'It was decided not to make a loan to a foreign diplomatic representative to pay allowances to his men'.[13] Donations of clothing and cigarettes were, however, allowed by the Red Cross. As the collapse of the 'Third Reich' drew closer, payments for the internees ceased completely. After considering the issue for several weeks and consulting Dr Hempel, the Irish government decided to permit the men to take on work in the area from May 1945 in order to earn some money and keep dissatisfaction at bay. The men found work in various spheres – for example as piano tuners, shoemakers, tailors, smiths, electricians or farm hands.[14] The willingness of the people of Kildare to give the men work was explained by the fact that they were pleased to have qualified workers (despite high unemployment figures it was often difficult to get qualified workers in Ireland) and secondly, it is probably correct to say that some Irish people were happy to help the soldiers, particularly when these soldiers had fought against England.

Some of the men who did not find work in the area started private 'companies' to earn money. A small bakery in the camp, a band which played at various functions and a shoe-making enterprise became very lucrative sources of money for some of the internees. Among other things, the soldiers bought bicycles, new suits and a radio from the money they earned.[15] One man commented later:

> We were treated in this camp well and with remarkable fairness. The guards had to perform their duty, of course, but they did it in a friendly manner. Moreover, most of them tried to do their best to make us feel at home as much as possible under those conditions.[16]

Thus the soldiers experienced comfortable conditions and hospitality from the Irish government and population during the war. From June 1945 however, the government was called upon by the Allies to send the internees back to Germany. In a letter of 14 June, 1945 from Sir John Maffey, British High Commissioner to Ireland, to the Secretary of the Irish Department of External Affairs, Joseph Walshe, the British made their position on the matter clear: 'Interned German Service Personnel' in Ireland were to be dealt with in the following way:

> Return as soon as possible to the British zone in Germany . . . They will be treated as ordinary disarmed German Service personnel on arrival in the British zone in Germany, and when disbanded, if their homes happen to be in the Russian zone, we could take no responsibility for their treatment there.[17]

The Irish government was not prepared to hand over the men without knowing how they would be treated. The following conditions were agreed with the Allies after the Irish government made it clear that it would not act without these guarantees:

1. That they would not be treated as prisoners of war.
2. That they would be sent direct to Germany.
3. That they would not be forced to go to the Russian-occupied zone against their will.[18]

When the men heard that they were to be sent back to Germany they reacted with varying degrees of relief or dread. Some were anxious to return to find out the fate of their loved ones; others had grown used to life in Ireland and feared conditions in Germany. Fifty did not want to return and applied for permission to stay. They were refused.[19] The Irish government was of the opinion that such a large number of foreign soldiers in Ireland as the result of a war could not stay in the country once the war had ended.

Three of the internees, Alfred Heizl, Rudolf Hengst and Josef Emmerich, married their Irish girlfriends after hearing this news, but were required to leave nonetheless.[20] Seven of the men fled the camp in the hope of avoiding deportation. All of them were caught, however, and sent back to Germany a little later than the others.

Only one of the soldiers managed to avoid being deported. His name was Georg Fleischmann and he had got to know some influential people, including Dan Breen, TD. He was able to use these people's help to stay in the country.[21] The fact that he was originally Austrian also helped him. He married an Irish woman and worked as a cameraman for RTÉ, for whom he often went abroad on government trips in the 1950s.

On 13 August the majority of the men were put on board a British ship and taken to Ostend. Instead of being taken directly to the British zone, as had been arranged with the British government, they were interned in a camp near Brussels, where they had to spend several months:

> In Ostend we were taken by US ammunition trucks to a POW camp near Brussels. There the Internees were kept as POWs for about 2 to 3 months, until released to their homes in Germany.[22]

The British government's promise was therefore not kept and de Valera's doubts about the treatment of the men confirmed.

ESPIONAGE IN IRELAND 1940–1941: A THREAT TO IRISH NEUTRALITY?

Alongside the fate of the internees, de Valera also had to arrive at a solution regarding the eight spies who were imprisoned in Ireland at the end of the war. As opposed to the internees, these men were accused of having committed crimes against Ireland. They were: Hermann Görtz, Werner Unland, Wilhelm Preetz (whose Irish wife lived in Bremen), Günther Schütz (alias Hans Marschner), Walter Simon (alias Karl Anderson) Ernst Weber-Drohl, Dieter Gärtner and Herbert Tributh. All of them, except for Werner Unland, had come to

Ireland to spy for Germany. Unland was interned because Schütz had named him as his contact in Dublin. He had fled England in 1939 and according to the Irish files was an out-and-out Nazi sympathiser – as late as 1945 he wrote a letter to the Irish government which he signed 'Heil Hitler'.

The other men, whose task was to spy in Ireland, had been badly informed about, and insufficiently prepared for, their mission:

> Due to sloppy planning and the Abwehr's poor intelligence about conditions in Ireland, with the exception of Görtz they were all picked up within days or even hours of landing.[23]

Dressed in unusual clothing and speaking with a foreign accent, they fell under suspicion easily, especially because the Irish took particular notice of foreigners in those days. It was a time in which the population was especially vigilant due to fears of a German or British invasion.

Ernst Weber-Drohl was to bring money to the IRA from Germany and transmit messages via radio. He landed in Ireland by submarine in the early days of February 1940, but lost his radio in the water while doing so. He managed to get the money to the IRA, however, before being arrested in Dublin in April 1940.

Walter Simon and Willy Preetz landed in Ireland in June 1940. They were both dropped by submarine at different locations in the south-west. They had been sent by Abwehr I, the spy division of the German secret service, and were to report on weather conditions and the movements of British ships in the Atlantic off the Irish coast.[24] Simon was arrested the same day by Irish detectives, Preetz a few weeks later. Preetz was not able to do more than send a few radio reports to Germany before being caught.

Two other men, Herbert Tributh and Dieter Gärtner, South Africans of German origin, were brought to Ireland by ship one month later together with an Indian named Henry Obed. They were even less successful in their mission than their predecessors. Having landed in Baltimore Bay, they set out to find the quickest way of getting to Dublin. The Garda report of a local man's meeting with the spies reads more like the script of a comedy than of a spy story:

> At about 7.30 am Patrick Geanery saw three men, two in overcoats and one in a white hat, standing on the roadway with their suitcases resting on the road. The elder of the three put up his hand and Geanery got off his cycle. 'Is this West Cork?', he asked.

Despite the obvious strangeness of this incident, and being spotted by several other local people, it wasn't until they were observed by a local Garda that they were arrested.

Günther Schütz worked for the Abwehr in Hamburg. He had spent one year – 1938 – as a student in England and had reported to the Abwehr on the economic situation in England since then. After the outbreak of war Schütz was used for various missions. He was sent to Spain, from where he made contact with Werner Unland. Unland had previously worked for the Abwehr and fled to Ireland with his English wife in 1939. Schütz was then given the task of spying in Ireland. He was parachuted in on 12 March, 1941 but was arrested the following day. Unland was arrested on 25 April, 1941 under the Emergency Powers Act, which was in force from September 1939 to September 1946. The police suspected him because of his previous contact with Schütz, and were not prepared to take risks. 'Not a single weather report which could have been useful to the Luftwaffe in their attacks on England could Admiral Canaris get from the Irish', a German news magazine, *Der Spiegel*, reported years later.[25]

There was one man whose story was different, and this was Dr Hermann Görtz. He landed on 5 May, 1940 by parachute. His mission was to gather information about the situation in Ireland, especially about the IRA, and if possible to promote trouble in Northern Ireland. After the war, Kurt Haller, then the leader of Abteilung I West (Abwehr II) in Berlin which was responsible for acts of sabotage and for dealing with dissatisfied minorities in other countries, told Conor Cruise O'Brien about the German interest in Ireland and their problems in carrying out plans:

> He [Haller] said that they wished to preserve contacts with underground elements here so as to be able the more easily to help resistance in the case of a British landing . . . The German Secret service had always had difficulties in its dealings with Ireland because of Dr Hempel's opposition to any activities of this kind.[26]

Haller described the motives of the German spies in such a way that the latter were presented as having no other mission than that of preparing for the eventuality of a British invasion. Görtz' task was not, however, to make preparations for such an invasion but, as mentioned above, to make contact with trouble-makers in Ireland. Görtz himself said:

> . . . I was to make it clear to the Irish that Germany was interested in
> a united independent Ireland. I could best prove the credibility of this
> assertion by myself actually fighting for this united Ireland.[27]

After Görtz had arrived in Ireland he made his way to the house of
Mrs Iseult Stuart, a sister of Seán MacBride, the former IRA leader.
She was the wife of Francis Stuart, who was lecturing in Berlin at the
time and whom Görtz had met before his departure for Ireland.[28] She
took Görtz in and gave him shelter without asking any questions.

Through Mrs Stuart the IRA found out about Görtz' presence in
Ireland and had him brought to Dublin.[29] There he met Stephan
Held, an IRA man who had been in Germany shortly before Görtz'
departure for Ireland in order to make contact with the Abwehr. Held
was arrested on 23 May in Dublin and items which belonged to
Görtz, including a typewriter and military details on Ireland, were
found in his house – a discovery that sparked off rumours that a
German invasion of Ireland was imminent.

Görtz managed to remain free until the end of November 1941,
during which time he made contact with some IRA members. Because
of the fact that the police were scouring the country for him, however,
he was unable to provide his superiors with any useful information or
to develop a concrete plan of action for Ireland. Apart from this, he
had formed the opinion that the IRA was badly organised and
therefore not useful for his purposes: 'I considered that the organisation was rotten at its roots'.[30] At no stage did he receive assistance
from the German legation. Indeed, the German Foreign Office had
warned the Supreme Command 'not to touch the IRA, as it would
inevitably lead to friction with the Éire government'.[31] On 27
November he was captured by the Gardaí. He spent the remainder of
the war in prison in Ireland.

The prison conditions for the German spies were not as generous
as for the internees, but they were not treated nearly as strictly as
ordinary prisoners. At first they were held in Mountjoy Prison in
Dublin and, according to Enno Stephan, their lives there was far from
unbearable:

> They were not living in narrow cells but in ordinary rooms in which
> the only alteration was that the windows were strongly barred. During
> the day they could move freely around the whole building. Their food
> was good. A warder brought them in extra provision if they wished.
> They all had enough money.[32]

Just how good conditions were was proven by the fact that Günther Schütz managed to escape, dressed in women's clothes which he had had brought to the prison. He was recaptured after two months. Following this event the men were taken to Athlone Prison to reduce their chances of escape.

In a report to de Valera (probably written by Dan Bryan, the head of the Irish secret service) one reason for treating the men well was named:

> One strong reason why small neutrals do not punish foreign agents with severity is the fact that they could not do so without screening themselves behind the other belligerent and becoming more dependent on it for future protection. They would, moreover, be exposed to the accusation of acting on behalf of the other belligerent . . . It is a generally accepted custom that small Powers in their international dealings should not take measures involving great Powers out of proportion to their capacity to defend themselves, whether by diplomatic or military methods.[33]

This attitude that it would not be appropriate to Ireland's position to punish the men severely was adhered to after the war, when the issue of the men's deportation arose. It was seen as very important by Irish politicians to maintain a line of action clearly independent of Britain.

THE FATE OF THE GERMANS: ALLIED ANGER

Allied impatience with Ireland had been growing during the war. The neutral stance had never really been accepted, the refusal to allow the Allies to use Irish ports was condemned, and the presence of German citizens in Ireland was seen as a threat. The perceived Irish stubbornness regarding the German legation in Dublin also contributed to this atmosphere of ill-will. As early as 21 February, 1944, David Gray, the American envoy to Dublin, had delivered a letter to the Irish government, in which his government demanded the immediate closure of the German and Japanese legations in Dublin.[34] De Valera refused to obey this request, which was formulated more as an order, as he refused to yield to most of the Allied requests concerning Germany.

The German ambassador, Hempel, continued to carry out his work in the legation until April 1945, although the final year of his duties was primarily taken up with looking after financial matters regarding

his staff and the German internees. In March 1945, as the collapse of
the German Reich drew nearer, pressure increased on the Irish
government to hand over the German legation building to the Allies.
The tone of these demands annoyed de Valera because they created
the impression that Ireland did not have the right to make an
independent decision in the matter. Gray showed his lack of
knowledge of Irish politics in his handling of the issue. The British
authorities knew better how badly such demands were received in
Ireland:

> Any step such as that contemplated by the Americans [to take control
> of the Legation] is of course a violation of Éire's neutrality. A legation
> is entitled to claim from the Government of the country to which it is
> accredited protection from any action threatening its diplomatic
> immunity . . . We can therefore expect the Éire Govt. to warn the
> Germans of our intentions.[35]

The British wanted the Irish authorities to have little warning of the
plan to take possession of the legation so that the Germans would not
be warned by them and so would not have time to destroy any files.

On 8 April, 1945 Hempel informed the Irish government that he
regarded his duties as a diplomat to be over in view of Germany's
collapse, and he handed over responsibility for the legation and its
contents to the Irish government.[36] Shortly before this the most
important files in the legation were indeed burned to ensure that they
would not fall into Allied hands. On 30 April John Maffey, British
representative in Ireland, met with de Valera and declared that he
wished to take possession of legation property in the name of the
Allies. De Valera refused to comply to this request before he had
consulted his legal department. Nothing could be done, he said, until
the war had officially ended. This issue contributed to the Allied
anger towards Ireland: 'We have also put upon record the refusal of
the Irish Government again to seize the opportunity of co-operating
with us in a friendly and non-legislative manner for allegedly internal
political reasons'[37] wrote Maffey.

Relations between Ireland and the Allies disimproved considerably
after de Valera paid Hempel a visit of condolence after Hitler's
suicide. De Valera was of the opinion that this step was necessary in
view of the country's neutrality, since he had paid Gray a similar visit
a few weeks earlier following Roosevelt's death. The decision was,
however, heavily criticised, both at home and abroad. De Valera
voiced his opinion on the matter thus:

I have noted that my call on the German Minister on the announcement of Hitler's death was played up to the utmost. I expected this. I could have had a diplomatic illness but, as you know, I would scorn that sort of thing . . . So long as we retained our diplomatic relations with Germany, to have failed to call upon the German representative would have been an act of unpardonable discourtesy to the German nation and to Dr Hempel himself . . . I was certainly not going to add to his humiliation in the hour of defeat.[38]

In view of the crimes committed by the National Socialist regime, many people were of the opinion that de Valera should indeed have availed of a 'diplomatic illness'. His visit to Hempel was an insult to those who had died in the Second World War and gave the false impression to the world that Ireland had in fact secretly been on the side of the Axis powers. This one action did more to decide foreign opinion on Ireland's role in the war than the careful years of neutrality preceding it. Two incidents in May 1945 contributed to a worsening of the strained relations. The first was a small anti-British demonstration which occurred in Dublin on 7 May after the German capitulation and which was reported by the British press as typical of the Irish reaction to the end of the war. The second was Churchill's speech on 13 May, in which he made some very bitter and insulting comments about Ireland's stance during the war.

In mid-May de Valera yielded on the question of the legation and permitted it to be handed over to the victorious Allies. Once in possession of the legation, Allied interest in its contents disappeared rapidly: 'We are doubtful whether any documents of value will be found. It has turned out that no one can be spared . . . to work on the archives of the German Legation at Dublin'[39] noted the British authorities. As in the matter of the German spies' deportation, which was the next issue to arise, the handing over of the legation had a symbolic rather than a practical value for the Allies. Their main concern was to have control over all German affairs in Ireland and not necessarily to gain information from this control.

The contents of the German legation, including Helmut Clissmann's private property which had been stored there for safe-keeping, were later auctioned in Belfast – after 'interested colleagues' from the American authorities in Ireland had chosen any items of use to them. Helmut Clissmann and Dr Heinrich Becker both confirmed that they later recognised these objects in private possession. An amount totalling £1,808 was raised at the auction and was paid into an American legation account 'for the payment of any expenses that may arise . . . and retained for eventual use in any German Consular Office here'.[40]

After the legation building had been handed over to the Allies, the latter concentrated on the staff of the German legation, all of whom had remained in Dublin. In June 1945 the Irish authorities received the first hints that the Allies wanted to question these people in Germany. Joseph Walshe wrote that the Irish government was not contemplating any forced deportation of the German minister or his staff:

> I told him [Maffey] the late German Minister was now a private individual residing here with his family and we did not consider it appropriate to take any steps to have him transferred to Germany until such time as he himself expressed a wish to go there . . . I did not give Maffey any hope that we would accede to any request to send the Legation personnel back to Germany without their complete agreement and goodwill.[41]

The number of staff involved was six: Dr Hempel, Henning Thomsen (legation counsellor), Johannes Bruchans, Wilhelm Müller (secretary) and two office staff. Carl-Heinz Petersen, a journalist, and Dr Heinrich Becker, a German teacher and cultural affairs expert, were also employed as freelance workers. They all stayed on in Ireland and tried to earn a living as best they could in the months after the war. Up to August 1945 they received their pay from Hempel. He used money which had been collected by the Irish government from German businessmen in Ireland to pay for the bomb damage caused by German warplanes. The Irish government had decided to loan Hempel some of this money so that he could fulfil his responsibilities towards his staff.[42] After this money ran out, the former staff earned their living in various ways. Mrs Hempel applied for permission to found a tailoring business. Although such enterprises were limited by the state at the time because of a shortage of material, and some Irish applications had already been refused, the Minister for Industry and Commerce decided that the Hempel's case was different:

> The Minister for Industry and Commerce felt that in the very special circumstances he would have to make an exception in her favour; we had hitherto refused all such applications from our own nationals.[43]

The Hempels decided, however, to open up a bakery instead, due to the difficulties in getting the material needed for the tailoring business. They were able to earn enough to feed their family of five children. Carl Petersen, who was married to an Irish woman, worked for a newspaper. Henning Thomsen earned his keep working for a construction company.[44] There is no information in the files on how Bruchans managed.

The exception which the Ministry for Industry and Commerce had been prepared to make for the Hempels illustrates the fact that the Irish authorities still felt they owed Hempel assistance and protection. The Allies, on the other hand, regarded him and his staff as enemies who had to be questioned about their activities. Thus further problems arose between the Allies and the Irish government over German matters. The British press took up the story in a sensationalist manner – 'Hitler's colony in Eire' was one of the favoured descriptions of the Germans in Ireland. Very little understanding was shown for the fact that the Irish government, and de Valera in particular, was still behaving in a neutral fashion in that they refused to acknowledge the war guilt of all Germans. In the course of discussions with de Valera on the matter of the diplomats, the American representative, Gray, declared that his country desired the improvement of its relations with Ireland, but that the behaviour of the Irish towards the Germans was making this difficult:

> I said that my government was urging cooperation because we felt that Ireland belonged in our world group and that we wanted her there but that it was very difficult for the United States Government to consider that Ireland was in fact with us as long as the Irish Government declined to accept the principle in question . . . we regretted Mr de Valera's recording himself in the group not cooperating with the United States and the United Nations.[45]

This was a time in which post-war world order was being constructed, and Ireland found itself in a very difficult position with the threat of international isolation looming. In October, Gray was ordered to inform the Irish Minister for External Affairs that America would not refuse to support the Irish application for membership in the United Nations (this was not successful until 1955 because of a Russian veto), but that the Irish attitude towards the fate of German diplomats and spies in Ireland was complicating matters:

> . . . the United States Government has supported the application of the Government of Éire for membership in the United Nations Organisation and will continue to do so . . . but the presence of Hitler's

officials, agents and supporters enjoying the protection of the government of Eire does not make easier the execution of such a policy.[46]

This declaration represented a considerable worsening of the relations between America and Ireland, which at this point had reached an historic low. Later, when Ireland was asked to join NATO but refused because of partition, this conflict in 1945–46 was still in the minds of the American authorities and contributed to their picture of Ireland as an isolationist state. De Valera decided in the immediate post-war period to sacrifice good relations with Britain and America for a demonstration of Irish independence.

Efforts to make the Irish comply with Allied requests continued throughout 1946. The British authorities found themselves in conflict with the Americans about the proper course to take with Dublin. They believed that the diplomatic staff did not represent any particular problem and wanted to concentrate on the deportation of the spies. They feared that the Americans would complicate the issue further if they dealt with it their way:

> The American State Department . . . is still treating the problem of both officials and agents as a whole, and is threatening, by somewhat heavy-handed action, to ruin our chances of success in either.[47]

After it had become clear that de Valera would not have the staff of the German legation deported, the British government decided to personally write to those concerned in the hope that they would return to Germany voluntarily.[48] Only the two secretaries, Ms Friedinger and Ms Lackkamp, replied that they were prepared to go back to Germany, the others all refused. Bruchans cited bad health as his reason for staying, Hempel his wife and five children whom he did not want to expose to the situation in Germany. Hempel also argued that in his opinion, Allied orders did not have any power in Ireland.[49] The reports from Germany about the deteriorating situation there, alongside the knowledge that they no longer had homes in Germany (Hempel could have only gone to a sister, Thomsen had heard that his farm had been confiscated) deterred them from returning to Germany voluntarily as long as they could stay in Dublin under relatively good conditions. The Allies did not want to deliver any promises as to what treatment awaited the diplomatic staff if they were to return to Germany,[50] just as they refused to make any clear statement regarding the fate of spies.

After this attempt to persuade the diplomatic staff to leave Ireland, the British and American authorities seem to have more or less dropped the issue. The Allies concentrated instead on the question of the spies, as the British had wanted. Hempel also played a role in this change of tactic. He had got involved in Görtz' case in that he attempted to convince him that he had nothing to fear from a return to Germany. Hempel met Görtz with Frederick Boland, and both tried to calm Görtz' fears, without success. The suspicion arises that Hempel saw the deportation of the spies as a way to distract Allied attention from himself. There is no official proof of this thesis, but it is certainly true that after the spies had been deported in 1947, the question of the diplomatic staff was not brought up by the Allies again. Before this was to happen, however, a lot of diplomatic and political wrangling had to take place. The Irish authorities had to consider the options open to them concerning the spies. The Irish secret service, G2, had been observing the men closely since their imprisonment. Colonel Dan Bryan was often consulted by the government on the matter. His advice was highly valued and his main concern was to ensure the greatest possible safety for Ireland in this difficult time. According to Dermot Keogh he was 'among the most intelligent, influential and pro-Allied officers to serve in the Irish army during World War II'.[51] When the war ended he advised the government: 'No undertaking [should] be entered into which would imply that any of those people will be allowed to permanently reside in this country'.[52]

Dan Bryan pointed out that the prisoners, if set free, would have to look for work in order to keep themselves. Bryan feared that Görtz would use his IRA contacts in order to earn money in some way, and called him 'a most persistent intriguer'.[53] Bryan feared the same thing regarding Günther Schütz, as he also had 'close IRA contacts'.[54] The possibility was also mentioned that Schütz could try to escape and portray Ireland in a bad light if questioned by the Allies in order to increase his chances of escaping punishment:

> Marschner [i.e. Schütz] is quite clearly a man of little character, and he is just the sort of person who might try to ingratiate himself with the Allied authorities by making false statements about German activities here during the war. Some people are still looking for that sort of material to use against us.[55]

Bryan also did not want Werner Unland to be allowed to stay in Ireland, although there was no proof that he had been involved in spying. De Valera did not, therefore, intend to grant these men permanent asylum. He was determined, however not to send them back to Germany straight away.

Some basic questions arise out of the issue of the German spies in Ireland: Why did de Valera refuse to have the men deported? To what extent did this refusal damage Irish post-war relations with Britain and America? What effect did the issue have on German-Irish relations?

Ireland and the Allies represented two completely different points of view on the question of the spies. The Allies demanded that the men should be handed over to them immediately. Sir John Maffey, British High Commissioner to Ireland, wrote:

> [they should] return as soon as possible to their own countries. We could give no undertaking that these prisoners would be immune, on return to their own countries, from punishment for any offences which they might have committed under their own domestic laws. [They] would be returned to the British zone in Germany and the Control Authorities would take them over then.[56]

J. P. Walshe, Secretary of External Affairs, wrote on 22 June, 1945, that he had informed John Maffey that the *internees* were to be sent back to Germany as soon as possible. The Irish government was not, however, prepared to deport the German *agents* as these had committed a crime against Ireland and therefore had to be kept in custody there. Only if the men wished to return to Germany voluntarily in the hope that they would be better off there would they be allowed to leave.[57] This disparity – arguing that the men were being detained for internal reasons while saying that they were free to leave the country – illustrates the fact that the delaying tactics of the Irish government mainly served one purpose, namely to show that the Allied demands for deportation were perceived as intruding on Irish sovereignty.

Walshe tried to find out from Maffey why the British were so determined to have the spies deported:

> I tried to ascertain from Maffey whether it was a question of getting information from these men, but he rather kept insisting on the political trouble that would arise from our keeping them . . . I frankly do not understand the British anxiety to get hold of them. The reasons given seem inadequate, but the fact that they do attach importance to the matter is borne out by the nature of the committee which specially

sat on the question when Maffey was in London last week. He told me
this morning that it was presided over by the Lord Chancellor and that
several of their important legal men were present.[58]

This statement illustrates that the British authorities were treating the
issue as a matter of principle, in the knowledge that they would
probably not actually gain any useful information from the men. The
issue led to tension in Irish–American and Irish–British relations –
indeed this was the first time that relations with America had reached
such a low. The importance of the Irish community in America was
not sufficient to alleviate the dissatisfaction of the American government with Ireland over this question, especially since Ireland had
already refused the American request during the war to be allowed to
use Irish harbours. The Irish government wanted to prove its independence to the rest of the world, and especially to Britain, by dealing
with the German spies as it saw fit. The Allies regarded the matter as
yet another instance of Ireland denying them cooperation in this
difficult time.

The situation was not improved by the behaviour of the American
ambassador to Ireland, David Gray. While Maffey hoped that the
prisoners would return to Germany voluntarily and was prepared to
wait for this to happen, David Gray condemned Ireland in strong
terms for its refusal to deport the men. He was of the opinion that
'Görtz and Co.' could provide the Allies with valuable information if
they could be questioned[59] and that they should be deported
immediately. The British wanted to act more diplomatically, as they
had in the matter of the diplomatic staff:

> The attitude of the United States Department is at the moment in
> danger of proving a very great embarrassment to us in the already
> delicate and difficult dealings with the Éire government.[60]

Compared to the cautious attitude of the British, the American policy
was much more determined. David Gray remained totally opposed to
the British policy of displaying patience. His attitude towards the Irish
government became increasing critical with time.

In June 1945, Görtz wrote a letter to the Irish Minister for Justice
requesting limited asylum in Ireland. He based his request on the
argument that his place of residence in Germany was in Potsdam and
that he would therefore fall into the hands of the Communists in the
case of his having to leave Ireland:

> If deported to Germany and handed over to the Bolsheviks according
> to the agreements between them and the British I have almost certainly
> to expect death from the Bolsheviks for military reasons.[61]

On 10 September, 1945, the Allied High Commission passed a
resolution that all German civil servants, agents or other 'obnoxious'
Germans were to be returned to Germany from neutral countries
immediately. Following this the pressure on the Irish government to
deport Germans from the country increased. At the same time, a
memorandum from the Department of Justice emphasised that the
imprisoned men no longer represented a threat to the security of the
country and went so far as to show understanding for the men:

> actuated by patriotic motives [they] undertook very dangerous tasks,
> and it would be improper to treat them in any way as if they were
> criminals . . . [but] The British and American governments . . . would
> regard it as an unfriendly act on our part to release the men without
> securing the agreement of the British and American governments to
> that course.[62]

A considerable difference of opinion arose between the Departments
of Justice and External Affairs on this matter. The latter was of the
opinion that the men should remain in prison, while the Department
of Justice spoke out in favour of their release. F. H. Boland from
External Affairs suggested the following changes to the report cited
above:

> . . . although not criminals in the ordinary sense, [they] were guilty of
> conduct amounting to a flagrant breach of our immigration laws and
> a complete disregard of our sovereign rights in circumstances gravely
> prejudicial to our national security . . . On the whole, the Department
> of External Affairs consider it better, not only from the point of view
> of the men themselves but of the other Germans still residing in this
> country, that the men should stay where they are for the present, and
> this is understood to be also the view of the staff of the former German
> Legation in Dublin.[63]

These two contrasting points of view indicate the basic differences
between the two departments. The Department of External Affairs
was in general more inclined to show understanding for the British
point of view than was the Department of Justice. In October 1945,
the decision was taken out of the hands of both departments when
the Taoiseach decided that the men should remain in prison. The

Allies, however, were not satisfied with this decision. They were still insisting on deportation. On 5 December David Gray sent a letter to de Valera, in which he again demanded deportation in the name of his government. De Valera replied that his government was prepared to help those men who wished to leave the country, but that 'the possibility of compelling German nationals . . . in order to join the millions of homeless outcasts now suffering cold and starvation in Europe, has not entered the contemplation of the Irish Government'.[64] Only one of the men, Walter Simon, chose to return to Germany, leaving in the winter of 1946. After a few weeks of interrogation in the British zone he was set free.[65] The pressure on de Valera mounted nonetheless. In March 1946 the French government also wrote to de Valera in order to protest at his refusal to hand over the men,[66] and the British press published a number of articles at this time about Ireland's willingness to shelter 'Nazis'.

Despite the demands, de Valera still refused to send the men to Germany. One of the reasons he gave to the Allies was that he would not be able to justify the move to the people of Ireland. Another was that the men had committed a crime against Ireland and would therefore have to remain in prison there.[67] De Valera wanted a guarantee from the Allies that the men would not receive high sentences, and on no account the death penalty, if sent to Germany. The British government was not prepared to deliver such a guarantee. Frederick Boland from the Department of External Affairs worked towards a compromise in the matter. He managed to secure a vague declaration from the British government that the men would not be sentenced to death:

> It has therefore now been tentatively proposed that Sir John Maffey should be authorised to tell the Éire authorities, for possible quotation in public, that so far as the United Kingdom authorities are aware, there are at present no charges against any of these men which would be likely to involve capital sentences.[68]

In spite of this, further complications followed. On the instructions of the Irish Department of Justice, the men were released on probation in September 1946, a move which was justified by the fact that they had been imprisoned under the Emergency Powers Act which had ceased to be in force in August 1946. The Department of External Affairs was not consulted on the decision, but received sharp criticism from the Allies because of the move: 'This . . . gesture by the Department of Justice embarrassed External Affairs and annoyed the

Allies.'[69] In the course of the war, Ireland's neutrality and David Gray's behaviour towards the Irish government had led to considerable coolness between America and Ireland. With this move the atmosphere grew even worse, as illustrated by the following statement:

> I am instructed to express . . . the deep regret of the Government of the United States that Your Excellency should choose so to exercise this right as to continue to shelter the paid servants and supporters of the infamous Hitler regime . . . it is difficult to conceive that Éire should not make the gesture of friendly co-operation with those who at great cost of blood and treasure have served Western civilisation and assured Irish freedom.[70]

The Irish government had to reach a decision whether to allow the men to remain free, in which case they would have run the risk that they would stay in Ireland permanently, or to rearrest them. From a legal point of view the men could only be returned to prison if a deportation order was served against them or if they were sentenced for a crime. Due to this legal problem, and to the fact that some time had passed since the Allies had first demanded the men, the Irish authorities decided that the only reasonable option open to them was deportation. There are some indications that the deportation of the spies at this time was carried out in order to protect the German diplomats in Dublin from similar demands that were being made by the Allies. It can be speculated that de Valera hoped to take the Allied pressure off the diplomats by deporting the spies. There is no official proof of this, only indications such as the following contained in a letter to de Valera:

> . . . to regard a group of professional spies as entitled to stay in this country would be to place ourselves in a position which we could not defend on logical grounds. Furthermore, such an attitude would be liable to re-open in an aggravated form the question of the continued stay in this country of the members of the staff of the former German Legation.[71]

The possibility was also mentioned by Robert Fisk in his study:

> There is even now a suspicion in Éire that Boland had been given a choice – to send either the spies or the diplomats back to Germany – and that Hempel had convinced the Irish that the agents should be returned in order to save himself.[72]

It is possible that this was one of several reasons which moved de Valera to his decision. Two main points influenced him: by 1947 he had let enough time go by to ensure that the prisoners would be treated more fairly after their deportation, and he had also proven that the Irish government was not prepared to react to pressure from Britain and America on matters it regarded as internal, a point on which de Valera placed considerable emphasis.

Wilhelm Preetz was the first to be deported on 15 April, 1947. He was taken to the British zone. Several articles in the Irish press reported that he had been deported due to Allied pressure on de Valera. As a result of this, the Department of External Affairs sent a letter to the foreign representatives in Ireland emphasising that this was not the case:

> It is not correct, as has been suggested in the Press, that the deportation of these men is the result of Allied pressure . . . [H]aving regard to the fact that nearly two years have elapsed since the termination of hostilities in Europe, it was considered that the time had come to require these men to return to their own country . . . It is particularly desirable to refute the malicious suggestion that the action was taken in consequence of pressure by other governments.[73]

The Irish government wanted to be sure that its independence in the matter was beyond doubt, having gone to such lengths to avoid just such an accusation.

Hermann Görtz, Werner Unland and Günther Schütz had all applied to stay in Ireland on asylum. In February, Görtz had become secretary of the 'Save the German Children Society', a society which was trying to enable German children to spend time in Ireland (see Chapter Three). Unland had continued with his business which he had run prior to his arrest. Both were thus able to argue that they could earn enough money to support themselves without requiring anything from the state. On 5 May, 1947, Görtz' application was nonetheless refused. He was given ten days in order to complete any business he might have. The Irish authorities had always tried to persuade Görtz that he had nothing to fear from his return to Germany. He did not believe them, however, and was convinced that his past would be used against him, since he had played a role in the suppression of the Spartacus movement after the First World War and had been a spy during the Second World War. He hated those in power in Germany and was afraid of the consequences of his behaviour:

Speaking with considerable heat and emphasis, he [Görtz] said that the Germans in authority in Germany at present were the scum of the country and that the main object of the Allies would be to crush out of existence people like himself who had worked for the greatness of Germany. He questioned whether the assurances given would be of much value in such an environment.[74]

Görtz was living in bygone days. He was not prepared to accept the fall of Nazi Germany or the new democratic leaders in the country. In his opinion, the only honourable solution to his fate was death. After being informed in the Aliens Office in Dublin on 23 May that he would be deported the following day, Görtz suddenly reached for his pocket, swallowed something and collapsed. He had taken poison. He died later the same day despite all attempts to save him and was buried on 26 May in Dean's Grange Cemetery in Dublin. Dr Hempel expressed the wish to attend the funeral but was advised against it by the Irish government and didn't go,[75] a decision which turned out to be a wise one as some IRA members were present, and a few of the mourners even gave the Nazi salute as the coffin was lowered into the ground. The British tabloid press used this event as further proof of their assertion that the Irish people had been, and still were, on Germany's side.

Gunther Schütz, who had been arrested the same day as Görtz, was deported on 26 June. He had been released on probation on 28 May in order to marry his fiancée, an Irish woman named Una Mackey. When he was deported his wife stayed in Dublin to wind up his business matters. In July 1947 she applied for permission to go to Germany to join her husband. She was permitted to do so, and Schütz set up an import–export company in Hamburg. The couple later returned to Ireland, but the marriage broke up some years later.[76]

Werner Unland and his wife were also to be deported but they threatened suicide after Görtz' death and were allowed to stay in Ireland. They made several attempts to obtain Irish citizenship. According to the Irish files on this case, which were kept up to 1961, their application was always refused.

Of the contentious German citizens, only some of the former diplomatic staff were still in Ireland by the end of 1947. Towards the end of 1948, Hempel himself decided to return to Germany. De Valera provided him with a reference about his time in Ireland which, de Valera hoped, would help Hempel to reestablish himself in Germany.[77] Hempel arranged to return on 20 May, 1949. The day before he left, he bade farewell to Gerald Boland (Minister of Justice), with whom he had got on well. This friendship highlights the good relations between Hempel and Irish politicians. In Germany, de Valera's reference did indeed help to have him exonerated from any crimes.[78] He received a salary from the Organisational Office for Consular Trade Representation Abroad at first. Within this organisation he was involved in the renewal of German diplomatic relations with Ireland in 1950. Hempel's two sons, Konstantin and Andreas, later returned to Ireland for a period in the 1960s.[79] Hempel himself visited Ireland in 1954, and his wife visited the country frequently, even after Hempel's death, as one of their children had died and been buried in Dublin. Johannes Bruchans left Ireland with his wife on 7 February, 1950, and returned to his home town of Freiburg. Before leaving, he expressed his thanks to the Irish authorities in a letter to the Department of External Affairs:

> I have much pleasure to express my sincerest thanks to you, the Department of External Affairs and all other authorities in Ireland for the great kindness which you and all officials have shown to me during my work with the former German Legation and especially after the closing down of the Legation.[80]

Henning Thomsen returned to Germany where, despite his behaviour in Ireland during the war, he was not prosecuted and went on to serve in the Foreign Service in Africa and Iceland in the 1950s.[81] No information is available in the files about the fate of the other legation employees after 1946.

RETURN TO IRELAND

For many of those who had, for whatever reason, found themselves in Ireland during the war, the country remained very important to them. Some of the internees who had been deported in 1945 actually returned after the Irish Ministry of Justice decided to grant permission to ex-internees who had Irish wives or fiancées to return to Ireland in February 1947.[82] According to the files, ten Germans applied for an entry visa, eight of them to return to their Irish wives or girlfriends and two of them to work in Ireland. At first the men were not permitted by the Allies to leave Germany, but in 1949 their exit visas were approved. T. Ryle Dwyer also writes about this period that some Irish women were allowed to go to their husbands in Germany in 1947, but he does not quote his source.[83]

The fact that some of the men were anxious to return to the country of their internment testifies to the bonds formed in their time spent there. While frustrated at being out of the war and missing their country, the men appreciated the good treatment they received by the Irish authorities. Arthur Voigt, for example, was allowed to return in 1949 to marry his fiancée, Miss Sheila McElroy. He had spent four and a half years in Ireland. He was sent back to Germany and lived for a time in Leipzig before fleeing to the British zone. After his marriage in Ireland, he settled in Co. Kildare. Another internee, Kurt Kyck, had married Elizabeth White, daughter of an Irish soldier and a woman from Cologne, before he left Ireland. (Her parents had met when her father had entered Cologne as part of the British army in 1919.) Kyck also returned to Ireland. A third man, Arthur Jackel, wrote that he was returning to Ireland because of his experiences during his internment: 'When I was in Ireland I had many Irish friends, and I loved the hospitable Éire.'[84] Walter Habicht, who had also been interned in the Curragh, stayed in contact with an Irish friend to whom he wrote about the conditions in Germany after he had fled from the Soviet zone with his family, and asked his friend for help. His letter shows the significance of Irish assistance for Germany:

> My wife is full of enthusiasm at the attitude of the Irish people. As a matter of fact the Irish have been the first to help us . . . For the time after the war she was the only nation who dared to show a kind attitude to the starving people.[85]

It can be said without a doubt that the treatment of these men during and after the war was humane and was not forgotten. This is especially true for those whose lives had been saved by the Irish ship *The Kerlogue*. This dramatic rescue took place after a naval battle in the Bay of Biscay. The 164 survivors spent up to thirty–six hours in the water before being picked up in a ten-hour operation by Captain Tom Donohue and his crew of nine and brought to Cóbh harbour. In May, 1994, a memorial service took place in the Maritime Museum in Dun Laoghaire to honour Captain Donohue and his crew for their bravery during the rescue in December 1943. Fifteen of those saved were present and one of them, Wolf Dietrich Klüber, thanked Ireland for the rescue and for the treatment which they received during their internment:

> They carried out a humanitarian operation of a very large scale in the middle of a cruel war. An act, which shall not be forgotten and live on

in history [sic]. Today, we also want to pay tribute to all those who helped us, cared for the wounded and sick. The doctors and nurses were dedicated and so were those who looked after all of us for more than 20 months of internment. We are grateful for all the care and attention we received.[86]

In Germany the men from the *Kerlogue* were also honoured when the two surviving crew members were invited to a memorial service in Eckernförde in 1995.[87]

One of the German participants in the Dun Laoghaire ceremony, Hellmut Karsch, wrote in a letter to the son of one of the survivors after the commemoration ceremony: 'The affinity of the Irish for Germany has to be emphasised. Once again we experienced warm hospitality'.[88] For these men the days of internment in Ireland were part of an experience which contributed to the strong relations existing between German and Irish people on a personal level:

> Many personal contacts have been maintained over the years – over almost half a century. A great number of the former internees of the German Internment Camp have visited your country again, most of them more often, many of them with their families. I can assure you that none of us will ever forget your country.[89]

THE GERMAN WAR CEMETERY

So far this chapter has dealt with German soldiers or spies who were in Ireland in 1945. A number of Germans also lost their lives in or near Ireland following plane crashes or shipwrecks. These were buried, some of them unidentified, where they were found. The Irish government donated wooden crosses for the graves.[90] Among the dead were eighty-one men from the Luftwaffe and the Navy, and forty-six civil prisoners who were drowned off the Irish coast when their ship, which was on its way from England to Canada, sank on 2 July, 1940.

In 1951, after diplomatic relations had been restored between Ireland and the Federal Republic of Germany, the German envoy, Dr Katzenberger, devoted his attention to these graves. After he had visited several of the sites, he determined that most of them were in a very bad condition since the Irish government had no funds available for the upkeep of the graves. A group of Irish people with German roots and Irish friends of Germany had attempted to take care of the graves, but the task was too large for them alone as the graves were scattered far apart.[91] Katzenberger suggested that the Volksbund Deutsche Kriegsgräberfürsorge, an organisation which looked after German graves all over the world, should take on the care of the graves in Ireland. The organisation proclaimed itself willing to do so if it received some financial assistance from the governments. It was suggested that the remains of the soldiers should be moved to a central cemetery in order to facilitate the care of the graves, identify missing soldiers and enable relatives to visit the graveyard. An agreement to this effect was signed by the Irish and German governments, whereby the Irish government placed a site in Glencree, Co. Wicklow, at the disposal of the organisation. The cemetery was built in 1959–60. The remains of one hundred and thirty–three soldiers from fifty–nine graves were exhumed and laid to rest there.[92]

Hermann Görtz was also buried in Glencree, but not until the 1970s due to political difficulties in the matter. His wife was determined that he should be buried there but met with resistance. Elisabeth Clissmann explained why this was so:

> It took a lot of manipulating because unfortunately there were certain types [from the German embassy] who were psychologically anxious to dissociate themselves from all that had happened. They didn't want to do anything that might annoy anybody, so since the question of Görtz' death was so painful they didn't want the whole thing touched.[93]

Finally those responsible agreed to the burial. Görtz' grave in Glencree is recognisable by a stone in the form of a sword, which Görtz himself had ground for this purpose.

At the entrance to the cemetery the following dedication can be read:

> It was for me to die
> under an Irish sky,
> there finding berth
> in good Irish earth.
> What I dreamed and planned
> bound me to my Fatherland
> But WAR sent me
> to sleep in Glencree
> Passion and pain
> were my loss – my gain
> Pray, as you pass,
> To make good my loss.

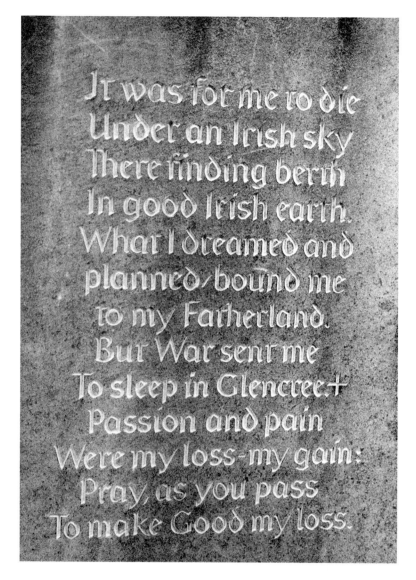

It was for me to die
Under an Irish sky
There finding berth
In good Irish earth.
What I dreamed and
planned, bound me
To my Fatherland.
But War sent me
To sleep in Glencree.✝
Passion and pain
Were my loss-my gain:
Pray, as you pass
To make Good my loss.

German cemetery in Glencree

The dedication was written by Professor Stan O'Brien who was very active in the Irish–German society. The graveyard is still very well maintained and relatives come there every year to commemorate their dead.

CHAPTER THREE

Humanitarian aid
after the war

GERMANY 1945

When the war ended in Europe, relief was mixed with unimaginable suffering on the part of many Europeans. In Germany this suffering was particularly acute. The total war effort that had led to the collapse of the country, together with the wave of refugees, expellees and returning soldiers brought the German people to the edge of starvation. The German people's fate depended largely on the policy of the Allied control powers.

The plan developed by the American Finance Minister, Henry J. Morgenthau, to punish and impoverish Germany and create a purely agrarian country (Morgenthau Plan), was the policy of the Allies from September 1944 to the Spring of 1945.[1] As the end of the war drew nearer and the political situation changed, the Allies distanced themselves from the plan. Instead of the Morgenthau Plan, JCS 1067 was the resolution that determined Allied policy at the end of the war. This resolution has been described as:

> a harsh and stern set of instructions largely negative in character . . .
> This directive showed the United States as a short-sighted country,
> motivated largely by revenge, and with little appreciation of the
> fundamental problems of an occupation.[2]

The reasons leading to the acceptance of this resolution by the Allies are understandable. Germany had committed crimes against humanity which were without comparison and had brought Europe to the edge of destruction. The Allies were not at this time inclined to show mercy to the German people. In reality, however, strict adherence to JCS 1067 would have meant that the Allies, and especially America, would have had to pump huge sums of money into Germany for an indefinite period of time.

General Clay, the American military governor in Germany, had to accept JCS 1067 as the governing resolution for Germany, but he did try to have it applied in a humanitarian way. In spite of the efforts made by the Allies and various charitable organisations, however, almost all the German people suffered from hunger, disease and lack of accommodation after the war.

IMMEDIATE AID FOR GERMANY

In the post-war period, Ireland was one of the first countries to assist Germany with donations of money and goods, even though the country was economically weak and the Irish people themselves faced rationing. The aid given saved many people from starvation and was an example of humanity shown in a very dark time in European history:

> The Irish people took on the suffering German people and our town [Freiburg] too and by their shining example of community spirit and sacrifice prepared the way for forgiveness between the peoples.[3]

> The thoughtful donations of the small Irish population represented an amazing achievement for the donators and considerable help for the recipients.[4]

The first assistance given to Germany by Ireland was in the form of medical staff. By June 1945, 250 doctors and nurses had responded to a request by the United Nations Relief and Rehabilitation Administration for fifty people to work in Germany and Austria.[5] This was part of a campaign by the UNRRA to put together 600 teams from neutral countries. The first three Irish doctors for Germany left on 1 August 1945.[6] On 4 October the Red Cross announced that it wanted to send food and medical supplies to Germany as quickly as possible in response to a plea by the International Red Cross for help for Germany. At this time it was difficult for the Red Cross to get assistance to where it was needed most, so the donations for Germany were directed through the International Committee of Catholic Charities as this organisation already had people working in most areas of Germany.[7]

Nevertheless, it was by no means easy to get aid to Germany quickly in the period immediately after the war, not least because there was initial reluctance to offering assistance to the former enemy. In America the charitable organisation CARE (Cooperative for American Remittances to Europe) was founded in November 1945 in order to help the peoples of Europe, but the Germans were not included in this assistance at first. Only from February 1946 did President Truman permit the transport of humanitarian aid to Germany, and the first CARE parcel didn't arrive in Germany until August 1946.[8] The Americans had realised that the German people would starve without foreign aid, and they also saw that permitting assistance for Germany would help to encourage democratic thought in the country.

Much of the Irish aid was sent to Germany via Switzerland. The American organisation National Catholic Welfare Conference (NCWC) provided the packaging material which was not available in Ireland, as well as financial and technical assistance in transporting the goods.[9] The Catholic Caritas organisation also took on the distribution of Irish goods, initially in all four zones of Germany. The goods were divided according to 'the size of the population of the individual zones and dioceses, the percentage of Catholic population, the degree of destruction and the number of refugees in each zone'.[10] Donations from Ireland were particularly large around Christmas; for example, in December 1947 the Irish people sent a donation worth almost two million dollars. The donations consisted mostly of beef products and clothing, but goods which the Irish did not have in abundance themselves because of rationing, such as sugar, were also sent.[11] The archbishop of München-Freising, Cardinal Faulhaber, expressed his thanks to the President of Ireland for the assistance:

> A new mass migration is occurring . . . expelled from their hearths and homes the refugees flooded over the border . . . More than ever we now rely on help from other countries. We are therefore deeply grateful to the people of the Irish Free State for sending . . . such generous donations.[12]

Donations from Ireland were per capita 'the highest donations from any country for post-war relief.'[13]

The Irish people did not receive only praise for their efforts to help the German nation. On occasion the accusation was raised, usually in English newspapers, that the Irish people were displaying a strange affinity for the Germans. The fact that public opinion in Britain was already very anti-Irish due to the country's neutrality during the war made it easier to make such accusations (see Chapter One). It can, however, be stated that the vast majority of those who donated for Germany did this for humanitarian reasons and not to support fascists or to provoke the Allies, as the accusations stated. The Irish people wanted to ease the lot of those who were suffering the most.

The general feeling in the country was that people should be deeply grateful that Ireland had been spared this suffering:

> The war has passed over the whole world and, excepting for a few brief moments of horror, has left our island undamaged. For this we have strong reason to be thankful.[14]

When the news of the expulsion of German populations from the East reached Ireland, the efforts to help the Germans increased. The memories which had been passed down of darker days in Irish history played a considerable role in this. One woman wrote to the *Irish Press*: 'With our own sorrowful heritage of the policy of "to hell or to Connacht", surely we will not exclude these unfortunate victims of war from our charity.'[15] Many years later – in the 1990s – Werner Friedrichs wrote the following about Irish aid: 'Their own traumatic past allowed the Irish in particular to empathise – they were remembering the suffering which the famine of one hundred years previously had brought to their country.'[16]

There were a few isolated cases in which hatred for England was a motive for wanting to help Germany. One example of such a view is a letter to the *Irish Times*, in which the writer asked why the 'well-nourished French' needed Irish help when the Germans were suffering so much: 'We can no more escape responsibility in this pressing matter [of the German people] than can the British, who declined to permit the Turks to help the starving Irish in the famine year of 1848.'[17] Such comments were seldom heard, but they did damage the Allied image of Ireland – and particularly that held by the British – and contributed to the difficulties in relations between Ireland and the Allies. They revealed an element of thought in Ireland that reacted against the spirit and realities of the time.

Many Irish people who had family or friends in Germany asked permission to send parcels to Germany, and the Irish government had nothing against this wish in principle. However, it was impossible to send private parcels to Germany in the immediate post-war period since there was no private parcel-postal service until 1949.[18] Donations for Germany could only be sent through official aid organisations. The journal of the Medical Association of Ireland called on the Irish people in October 1945 to send goods, wherever possible, to Germany. The reasons for this appeal were explained in the article:

> We realise that the sending of food to Germany especially may be fraught with many difficulties, but, if the need is great, we trust that

aid will be sent wherever charity directs. Apparently the food situation of certain parts of Germany is extremely bad. Let us do all we can to prevent this being the worst European winter since the Thirty Years War.[19]

The Irish Red Cross voted in March 1946 that three-fifths of a sum of £5,000 that was to go to the International Red Cross should be spent on Germany, one-fifth on Austria and one-fifth on Yugoslavia.[20] In every post-office in the country there was a list of suitable food donations to ensure that the right things would be given.[21]

Ireland as a refugee destination

Although the Irish people were more than willing to provide assistance for Europe, the country was not a noticeable destination for refugees. In the time before and during the war, Ireland was just as closed to refugees, including European Jews, as most other countries. The Jewish Museum in Dublin wrote about this issue:

> There is little to celebrate in the account of Irish policy towards Jews prior to and during the Emergency. In truth, there was bureaucratic indifference and a complete lack of concern by the general public tinged with anti-Semitism.[22]

After the war there were signs at first that Ireland would, in general, remain closed to refugees, but this policy was fortunately replaced by a more generous one:

> There was considerable resistance, particularly from the Departments of Justice and Industry and Commerce, to the idea of the government adopting a liberal refugee policy, but the Departments of the Taoiseach and External Affairs ultimately secured a more open approach . . . Ireland's role, however, remained far from exemplary.[23]

In the years immediately after the war the numbers of refugees remained low despite the relatively liberal policy of the Department of External Affairs. Ireland tended to concentrate on sending goods to Europe rather than taking in refugees.

Some Germans did manage to emigrate to Ireland after the war, and one of the most prominent of these was Prince Ernst Heinrich of Saxony, the third son of the last Saxon King. He decided to leave Germany because, in his words, 'I did not want to stay in Germany after the loss of my beautiful Castle Moritzburg'[24]. He chose Ireland, having heard of the advantages the country had to offer: 'I knew of the empathy with Germany and the price of land was low in comparison with the other European states.'[25] The Irish hospitality of which he had heard did not disappoint him. He quickly received a permanent residence permit and bought property in County Westmeath, where he lived with his family until his death in 1971. In Germany, Ireland slowly became a popular destination in certain circles, and a small number of Prussian aristocrats, most of whom had lost their land in the former Eastern Provinces, moved to the country in the 1960s to live as landowners.

A dramatic attempt was made by fifteen German POWs to gain refuge in Ireland in January 1946. The prisoners, having escaped from a military ship in France, landed in Co. Cork in the hope that they would be treated as refugees and sent to Germany by the Irish government: 'We believed that the Irish people, who were neutral in the war, would deliver us back to our homeland.'[26] In this case, however, the government could not consider the men to be refugees and therefore returned them to France on 8 February.[27]

In two separate incidents in 1951, two boats with refugees on board fled from the Russian zone of Germany and made for Ireland. The first boat, with a family of eight on board, landed in Rosslare in January 1951. The *Irish Times* wrote of the captain of the ship: 'He had worked in the Soviet zone of Germany, but wanted to get his family away from the Russians . . . [He had] heard much about Irish hospitality'.[28] A few months later, in June 1951, the yacht *Sea Wolf* arrived in Ireland with fifteen refugees on board: 'Kunath [the captain] was threatened with imprisonment [in Russia] because he refused to work for the Communists and he thus became one of the main movers for the escape.'[29] Both groups of refugees were at first taken care of by the Red Cross. After spending six months in Ireland, the *Sea Wolf* was rebuilt into a fishing boat with the help of the Red Cross in order to be used to earn money.[30] The refugees were granted residence permits and, from the Irish files, it appears that they stayed in Ireland, at least for some years.

THE SAVE THE GERMAN CHILDREN SOCIETY – A CONTROVERSIAL ORGANISATION

As described in the beginning of this chapter, public opinion in Ireland in 1945 led to considerable assistance being given to Germany. This atmosphere led not only to large donations, but also to the foundation of the Save the German Children Society on 16 October, 1945, in Dublin. This organisation played an important, and sometimes controversial role, in Irish post-war aid for Germany.

The Society was founded by Dr Kathleen Murphy 'in the hope of forming a society to save as many German children as possible from death by starvation this winter.'[31] In response to the question why the Society wanted to help German children in particular, Dr Murphy answered that they were the ones who needed the most help, and that she as a Christian saw it as her duty to do so. It was unfortunate that on the evening of the first meeting some of the members expressed other reasons for helping German children. One of them, Kevin Cahill, gave as his reason for wanting to help: 'Whatever measure of freedom [we] got in this country, [we] got with the aid of guns that came from Germany'.[32] Colonel J. J. O'Byrne expressed his thoughts in even more radical terms. He said that he was supporting the Society

> on the grounds of [my] pro-German feelings and [my] hatred of Britain. [We] should do everything possible to end the Anglo-Saxon influence, not only here, but elsewhere. If [we] took those German children, [we] should see that they are brought up as Germans, and do not come under Anglo-Saxon influence.[33]

Such comments resulted in the organisation immediately gaining a bad reputation in official circles, both at home and abroad. After having been put under a lot of pressure for remaining neutral in the war, and with the argument about the fate of German spies and diplomats in Ireland in full swing, the Irish government did not need the presence of a society that could be accused of being pro-German and anti-British.

The Society advertised successfully by means of posters, advertisements and leaflets for Irish host families.[34] The political comments did not affect the number of offers which came in to foster German children. From interviews conducted it can be deduced that those families willing to help did not want to do so because of the political opinions expressed but because of purely humanitarian reasons. Later on, however, when the Society tried to have the children brought to Ireland with the help of the British government and the Irish Red Cross, the comments were to have a negative effect since the Society had been labelled fascist by the authorities.

There is no doubt that comments such as those cited above were nationalist, anti-British and out of place, especially given the background of war. It is understandable that some Irish and British authorities regarded the Society with scepticism. Only a small minority of the members identified with such political comments, however. Most of them genuinely wanted to assist Germany. Dr Murphy expressed her opinion about some of the founding members of the Society in an attempt to ban politics from the Save the German Children Society and distance herself from the anti-British comments:

> they [the committee members] did not wish to instil hatred in anybody and had no political motive, and their main objective was to save the children from starvation. The views expressed by the speakers were not the views of the committee.[35]

Despite this, it was too late to save the Society's reputation with the authorities. The anti-British comments were documented in a secret police report which was given to the Department of External Affairs.[36] According to this report, one man, Kevin Cahill, actually called out 'Heil dem Führer' at the end of his speech to the members. It was also noted that some of the members had had contact with the German soldiers who had escaped from the Curragh in 1945 (see Chapter One).[37]

On 18 October, 1945, the Fine Gael TD Oliver Flanagan posed a question in the Dáil, asking when German children could be brought to Ireland and parcels sent to Germany.[38] This question cannot be regarded as a simple attempt to help German children with no political motive, given Flanagan's political record – he had made a name for himself as an anti-Semite during the war. In 1943, for example, he asked the government why it had not taken special measures against 'the Jews who crucified our Saviour 1900 years ago and who are crucifying us every day of the week'.[39] It is not clear whether Flanagan was directly involved in the Save the German Children Society or not. He did, however, try to pave the way for German children to come to Ireland in that he represented the wishes of some of his constituents to adopt German children to the government.[40] The fact that he actively supported the aim of the Society can only have damaged its reputation in the eyes of the government. In response to his question in the Dáil, he was given the cautious answer that the government was already giving aid through the Red Cross and that it was difficult to enable children to come to Ireland at the time.[41] Dan Breen, a Fianna Fáil TD who was active in the society,[42] was also of dubious character regarding his attitude to Jews. He had often visited the German embassy during the war and was critical of his Jewish party colleague Robert Briscoe.[43]

The anti-British comments that had been expressed at the founding meeting of the Save the German Children Society were strongly criticised by the *Irish Times*. One of the newspaper's correspondents labelled the meeting 'a thinly veiled excuse for the dissemination of Fascist propaganda'.[44] Dr Kathleen Murphy denied that the Society was interested in fascism:

> the Committee of the Save the German Children Society have (sic) at least one thing in common with [the correspondent of the Irish Times], and that is that they have no desire to see an infant's school of Nazism set up in their midst . . . [W]e have selected the German children as the object of our interest and charity, because, beyond all question, they are the most necessitous.[45]

The Irish Save the German Children Society was not the only one that was trying to help German children at the time. There were organisations in England, Sweden, Switzerland, Denmark and South Africa that were trying to have German children brought to their countries. However, because of the history of German assistance for Ireland's fight for independence, Ireland's neutrality during the war and the political statements of some of the members of the Save the German Children Society, the Irish organisation was regarded with distrust by the Allies in comparison with other such organisations.

OBSTACLES TO HUMANITARIAN AID

Disagreement with the Red Cross

After the foundation of the Save the German Children Society there followed a period of frustration for those who genuinely wanted to help German children. Up to December 1945 the Society had received 280 offers from families to foster children and had collected £620. Although Polish and French children had arrived in Ireland through the Red Cross, the Save the German Children Society was no closer to getting German children into Ireland than it had been in October.[46] The press began to show considerable interest in the matter. In December several articles appeared in the *Irish Independent* which criticised the slowness of the government in bringing German children to Ireland.[47]

In these articles the first signs of dissatisfaction on the part of the Save the German Children Society with the Irish Red Cross became apparent. The accusation was raised that the Society had not received a satisfactory answer from the Red Cross regarding the suggested co-operation between the two,[48] and that the Red Cross was merely waiting for the government to take up the matter instead of doing something about it itself.[49] The Red Cross for its part distanced itself from the Society, its spokesperson declaring: 'I should state that the society which appealed on behalf of German children is a distinct body from the Irish Red Cross'.[50]

In January 1946 a representative of the Red Cross, Mrs Hackett, travelled to Freiburg and Geneva in order to observe the relief work for Germany. She said at a press conference after her return that the aid situation in Germany was very difficult, since the German Red Cross no longer existed. Distribution of goods was carried out by the Caritas organisation and the Relief Action of the Evangelic Churches, she reported. She also stated that the Allies would not, to the best of her knowledge, permit German children to travel to Ireland.[51] The Save the German Children Society, on hearing this news, redoubled its efforts to get children to Ireland. The committee sent the following telegram to the United Nations:

> In the interests of Christian charity and world peace, we appeal to UNO to allow the starving German children to be taken to Ireland from Germany to avail of the 500 homes offered them here under the auspices of Save the German Children Society.[52]

The Save the German Children Society also continued to try to enable children to travel to Ireland by attempting to gain the assistance of the Red Cross. Up to the beginning of 1946 the answer remained the same – that the Red Cross could do nothing as the matter was being controlled by the Allies.[53]

Further difficulties – the Irish and Allied governments

On 30 January, 1946, Isolde Farrell, the secretary of the Save the German Children Society, went to the Irish Department of External Affairs and requested a declaration, which she was given, that the Irish government would grant an entry visa for German children if the Allies were to allow them to leave Germany.[54] Shortly afterwards the Irish government was informed by the British Representatives Office that there were in principle no objections to allowing German children to travel to neutral countries, but that there were several practical difficulties, especially regarding transport. In this letter it was again emphasised that the Red Cross would be permitted to supervise such a project, but that the Save the German Children Society was to be kept out of the plan:

> The 'Save the German Children Society' have (sic) done a great deal of harm by the political character of the speeches at some of their public meetings and by allocating all the offices in the Society to persons of well-known pro-German sympathy.[55]

It was highly unlikely that the Allies would approve a plan submitted by this society, continued the letter. Further, the attempts by the Irish government to channel the activities of the Save the German Children Society through the Red Cross were praised. In this, the consequences of the political atmosphere created at the Society's first meeting became apparent. The politicisation, together with the negative attitude in Britain towards Irish relations with Germany, made it very difficult for the members to make progress in their work. Enno Stephan has confirmed this fact:

> I know that they experienced considerable difficulties to achieve anything at all in the hostile atmosphere of the time which was felt against Germany everywhere.[56]

Finally, the British letter recommended that persons who had expressed an interest in fostering a German child should be directed to the Red Cross, but by no means to the Save the German Children Society.

On 19 February, 1946, a meeting of the Save the German Children Society took place in which an attempt was made to improve the Society's image. The main speaker, Stuart Morris from a pacifist organisation called the Peace Pledge Union, described the situation in Germany and called on those responsible to save German children from starvation.[57] Dr Proinnsias O'Sullivan, director of the Save the German Children Society, then named his reasons for wanting to support the efforts being made:

1. This is the first time in history that Ireland is again a nation after 700 years.
2. Because Ireland owes the German nation a debt of gratitude, not political gratitude, but gratitude to the group of scholars in Würzburg who revived the Irish language.
3. Because the greater part of Germany was evangelised by Irish monks who went abroad like seagulls to spread the light of faith.[58]

The fact that he mentioned Irish independence at an event which was supposed to be purely humanitarian, however, weakened his argument that politics should not play a role in the Society.

At the meeting the decision was made to ask the Allies again to allow German children to be sent to Ireland. A telegram to this effect was sent to the French and American embassies and to the British representative in Ireland. These answered that the Society should write to the Irish Department of External Affairs, so that they in turn could address the Allies on its behalf. In response to this a letter was sent to the Department on 8 March, 1946.[59] This letter was ignored by the Irish government in favour of a Red Cross offer to take on 100 German children. On 16 March Joseph Walshe from External Affairs wrote to the British representative that his government would approve the entry of the children if this was supervised by the Red Cross.[60]

At the same time, an application for exit visas from the British zone for German children was being examined by the British authorities. The application had at first been refused because a similar request by British citizens in 1945 had been rejected. This plan had not been allowed to go ahead because '. . . it would have meant doing more for Germans than we have done for our Allies.'[61] The British Foreign Office admitted, however, that the Irish offer could not be turned down for this reason:

> But that is an entirely different thing from preventing the Irish from rescuing some German children from starvation. [The] objection that this would prevent the re-education of German youth on democratic lines seems to me so fantastically idiotic that one is at a loss for comment.[62]

The arguments of those authorities in Britain who wanted to prevent German children from travelling to Ireland were rejected in the face of the continuing suffering in Germany. The British authorities declared themselves willing to allow German children to leave their zone. For the members of the Save the German Children Society, however, this did not mean that the children could come under the auspices of their Society. On 25 May, 1946, the Secretary of the Control Council for Germany and Austria wrote to the Save the German Children Society to say that he needed more information, e.g. about transport arrangements, before he could accomplish anything for them. In contrast to this, the Red Cross received the news that it could take on 100 German children on 31 May. The Irish government emphasised: 'it is especially desirable that there should be no publicity regarding the matter until the arrangements have reached their final stage.'[63] It would seem logical to assume that the government desired secrecy so that the Save the German Children Society would not hear about the plans for the 100 children and so would not get involved. The British authorities certainly were still not convinced that cooperation with the Society was advisable. A new pre-condition to its inclusion was introduced: only if a guarantee could be obtained that the children would return to Germany after a certain period would permission be granted to the Save the German Children Society to take care of them. Otherwise, according to the authorities, the suspicion would arise 'that we are promoting the foundation of a new German colony in Eire'.[64] Those responsible declared that they suspected the Society was planning to have the children adopted and were against such a move since they feared that it would mean a worrying increase in the number of Germans in Ireland. This was only one of many objections raised, however. The real reason for British doubts was still the political character of a few of the members' declarations.[65]

The Save the German Children Society also tried to gain support for its plans on a regional level. For example, the committee wrote to Limerick Council to ask it to support the work being done by the Society. The Council did not comply with this request, however:

> It seems that this benevolent Society wants to billet an unspecified number of young Teutons on people in this country, but cannot get them here without the consent of the Allied Council . . . Ireland owes infinitely more to France, Italy and Belgium than to Germany . . . The resolution would have a better chance of approval if framed to include children of all the countries in need of succour.[66]

The City of Limerick thus gave generous assistance to the Red Cross but not to the Save the German Children Society. Some individuals and institutions, such as Crescent College, were, however, involved in taking on children once they had arrived.

A certain amount of cooperation did take place between the Red Cross and the Save the German Children Society. In June, 1946, the Society in Cork sent a donation of clothes to the Red Cross in Dublin so that the latter could have them distributed in Germany.[67] Around this time, a meeting also took place between representatives of the Red Cross and of the Save the German Children Society in Dublin.[68] Dr O'Sullivan declared, in the name of his organisation, that they were unable to finance the costs of transportation for German children to come to Ireland. The Red Cross suggested that the Save the German Children Society should take on the first group of 100 children and that it, the Red Cross, would cover the costs of the transport. Cooperation on the matter seemed to be finally working. A government report dated the following day, however, re-emphasised that the government would not support the activities of the Save the German Children Society:

> From remarks dropped by members of the British Legation here, we feel that the activities of the Save the German Children Society are not improving the chances of getting German children to this country, and, therefore, that the more the matter is left in the hands of the Red Cross, the better.[69]

This point of view was confirmed by the Department of External Affairs:

> The British, on whose consent we depend to get children from Germany, do not feel well disposed towards the Save the German Children Society which they suspect of political motives.[70]

SUCCESS – OPERATION SHAMROCK

The arrival

On 4 June 1946, Isolde Farrell wrote to the Department of External Affairs in order to inform the Minister that the Red Cross would take on the costs of transporting children to Ireland for the Save the German Children Society.[71] This cooperation was confirmed in a Red Cross report:

> Arising out of the meeting of the deputation with members of the Executive Committee on 3.6.1946 it was agreed that the Red Cross would pay the cost of the transport of 100 children and keep them up to 10 days at Glencree, all other matters to be the responsibility of the 'Save the German Children Society.[72]

On 29 June, 1946, a meeting took place between representatives of External Affairs, the Red Cross and the Save the German Children Society. Conor Cremin, Secretary of External Affairs, wanted to know more details about the plans that the Society had made in order to ensure that the children would go to suitable families. Dr Murphy replied that her Society wanted to put the children up in respectable families: 90% of the children were to go to Catholic homes and 10% to Protestant homes. (The organisation also had six offers from Northern Ireland to take on children.)[73] Jewish children were not desired, it was stated.[74] Although there were a small number of anti-Semites in Ireland at this time, it is unlikely that direct anti-Semitism was at the bottom of this attitude. It is more likely that Catholic families were not prepared to take on Jewish children because of lack of knowledge about the religion and lifestyle. Catholicism at the time strongly embraced many aspects of family life in Ireland and so it would have been difficult to bring up a child of another faith in such an atmosphere. Given the knowledge of the horrors in Europe, however, to refuse Jewish children was an unchristian and politically dubious move.

Cremin explained at the joint meeting that the government required a list of the prospective families. The foster-parents had to sign a declaration regarding the care of the children, and the government sought assurance that all houses would be inspected before the children arrived should the Save the German Children Society be allowed to carry out its plans.

Shortly after the meeting, the Minister for External Affairs informed the Minster for Justice that 500 German children were to receive exit visas from the Allied Control Council. While it was emphasised that the children were to be allowed to enter Ireland, the Secretary of External Affairs noted that the Save the German Children Society was by no means to carry the sole responsibility for the children. He recommended cooperation between this organisation and the Irish Red Cross.[75]

There then followed a further setback for the Society due to the fact that the Department of Justice did not agree with the opinion voiced by the Department of External Affairs. The former was completely against the idea of the Save the German Children Society having any responsibility for the children:

> [we] would be opposed to the Save the German Children Society being allowed to arrange for the admission of children and their placing in homes here; the Minister for Justice feels that work of this kind should only be entrusted to a permanent, recognised body such as the Irish Red Cross Society.[76]

The Department of Justice recommended that External Affairs advise the Society against its activities. If the members were to ignore this advice, it was suggested that the British authorities 'intimate that the Society does not offer sufficient safeguards in the way of organisation and permanence to enable them to send children from Germany to the Society.'[77]

Early in July 1946, two representatives of the Irish Red Cross, O'Connor and Gallagher, went to England to discuss transportation details with their British counterparts. The latter emphasised that they would prefer to work directly with the Irish Red Cross than with the Save the German Children Society. The representatives of the Irish Red Cross observed that 'the Save the German Children Society was regarded with suspicion and as a semi-political organisation.'[78]

At the end of June the bureaucratic obstacles had been overcome and it was possible to permit children to come to Ireland. On 27 July, 1946, the first children – eighty-eight in all – arrived in Ireland as part of an action named 'Operation Shamrock'. The Save the German Children Society was not officially informed of the arrival or invited to participate in it.

The previous day, Miss O'Farrell and Miss Kilcullen from the Save the German Children Society had gone to the Department of External Affairs. They had requested a letter of introduction from the Minister for an impending visit to Britain, during which they wished to visit the authorities involved. They did not, however, receive such a letter since the Department feared that this would seem like an official recommendation of the Society. Conor Cremin described his impression of the visit thus:

> that she [Miss Kilcullen] would not deny that the Society is making the present arrangements only because Germany is in such a bad political situation and not primarily because German children are badly off . . . that if Germany should be politically rehabilitated tomorrow, the interest of the members of the Society in German children, even though they should still be suffering, would quickly wane.[79]

After two groups of German children had arrived in Ireland without its participation, the Save the German Children Society wrote to the Red Cross requesting it to bring 530 children to Ireland on its behalf, since it had enough accommodation for this amount.[80] The Red Cross informed the government of this request and Martin McNamara, head of the Red Cross, wrote that his organisation probably would not agree to transport children for the Save the German Children Society.[81] He also wrote that the Red Cross was considering advertising in newspapers for homes for German children – in other words, it was planning to completely exclude the Save the German Children Society from the humanitarian work, despite the agreement reached in June 1946.

The Save the German Children Society was very bitter about the rejection of its efforts:

> It should have followed that the organisation that had put in all the work should get the fruits of its labours but the F. F. government decreed that its nominated body the Irish Red Cross Society should enjoy the publicity now that there was no likelihood of offending the control powers . . . Since then the IRC Society has controlled all charitable dealings with Germany and the ISGC Society must remit assistance through it.[82]

This is what a member of the Save the German Children Society wrote in a private letter in 1949. The Society's work had nevertheless not been in vain. It had prepared the way for the acceptance of German children in Ireland by its insistence on carrying through the matter. Without the permanent questions and requests by the Society, the efforts would probably have been dropped or at least postponed, which would have meant further suffering for the children. The Society was also allowed to have a hand in taking care of the children in the end. It can, in any case, be said that the organisation paved the way for Irish aid for German children after the war.

Caring for the children

By 25 October, 1946, there were 190 German children in Ireland. Of these 134 had already found homes with Irish families.[83] Years later, one of them, Ernest Berkenheier, gave the following account of his arrival in Dublin: 'As we got off the boat at Dún Laoghaire the pier was lined with tables, covered with white sheets, lots of Red Cross nurses standing behind serving out cocoa and bread with lots of butter on.'[84] Paradise for the children of war-shattered Germany!

Later, as the harsh winter began, 126 more children arrived. On 15 November the Red Cross informed the press that all the German children in Ireland were their responsibility, but that they were cooperating with the Save the German Children Society.[85] There are no further precise details about how the children were distributed to the homes and whether this was done by the Save the German Children Society or by the Red Cross. The evidence found in the files and conversations with those involved indicate that both organisations were involved in the care of the children.

By 2 April, 1947, there were 418 German children in Ireland.[86] They had been chosen mainly by the German Caritas organisation

Group of German children arriving.
(Photo courtesy of Ute Carey née Schäfer)

and the majority of them were from the Ruhr area, which had suffered intensely from the Allied bombing campaign.[87] It was also an area with a high Catholic population. Some of the children were orphans, but most of them had one or both parents who were unable to take care of them. They were aged between three and fifteen years, the youngest children often being accompanied by older siblings. When they arrived in Ireland most of them were first taken to Glencree in Co. Wicklow, a few going to other centres in Co. Louth or Co. Donegal, where they were taken care of by nurses and Red Cross workers. Interpreters were present to overcome the language barrier. The following is a description of the initial phase of the children's stay in Ireland:

> When the children arrive in Ireland we take them to St Kevin's in Wicklow where we keep them under medical observation and build up their strength through nourishing food or a careful diet. Then they go to families, who raise and educate them with their own children and provide for their spiritual well-being. Each child is fostered by a family of the same religion. The Irish Red Cross has total responsibility for the children.[88]

Once they had physically recovered, they were chosen by foster parents. In order not to separate brothers and sisters, some Irish families took on two or even three German children, as one woman, Ursula Weber, described:

> As twins, we were determined not to be separated. I saw a kind-looking woman and pulled at her sleeve. She immediately said she would take me. I pulled my sister towards me. The woman looked at us and nodded.[89]

The way in which distribution occurred – the children were literally lined up for selection – was thus very haphazard, with no involvement on the part of workers in determining if the children and the families were suitable for each other.

Distribution took place throughout the country, but there were areas where a lot of children were centred due to the particular efforts made by the residents. The Jesuit Crescent College school in Limerick, for example, organised collections for German children in 1947 and also enrolled children in the school when they had been taken in by local families. These efforts were encouraged by a priest in the school who originally came from Aachen.[90] The then TD for North Kerry, Paddy Finnucan, arranged for twenty children to be fostered in his constituency.[91] In Dublin the suburbs of Rathgar, Rathmines, Ranelagh and Terenure were very active in the campaign. These areas were also centres of German–Irish relations on other levels. Several of the German spies had hidden out there, for example, and after the war cultural relations between Germany and Ireland were encouraged strongly by people from these areas.

The efforts to help German children continued in 1948 as the situation in Germany had not improved; indeed, in many areas returning POWs and refugees had exacerbated the problems. On 15 October, 1948, 100 children from Paderborn arrived in Glencree, not to be fostered but to spend a prolonged holiday in the countryside.[92] They stayed in Ireland until 28 March 1949 on a recovery holiday, during which time their health improved considerably.[93]

The Save the German Children Society was still active. It kept in touch with the children to ensure that they were happy and well taken care of and to sort out any problems which arose.[94] A large majority of the children got used to life in Ireland very quickly – so much so that the younger ones forgot the German language and spoke only English and, in some cases, fluent Irish. In order to refresh their knowledge and make the later transition back to German life easier, German courses were provided for them in Dublin. St Kilians, a German school which developed from these roots, still exists today. (In an interesting quirk of fate, one of the children who arrived in 1946, Uta Schäfer, stayed in Ireland and now is herself a teacher at St Kilians.) The funds for the German lessons were raised by the Save the German Children Society and by the Irish legation in Bonn.[95] The school was first located at 44 Leeson Park, where the Irish–German Society and the German Girl's Club (a club for German girls working in Dublin) were housed. Those who were responsible for the children made a big effort to ensure that they did not lose their sense of being German. There is no evidence to suggest that the children were influenced politically to become young Irish rebels or German fascists, as some British authorities had feared.

Not all of the stories had a happy end, however. In the course of the research done for this book, two cases were revealed in which a child was abused by its foster parents. One of these was Franz Othengraf, who was taken in by a farmer near Dundalk and put to work doing heavy manual work on the farm despite his age. As soon as this became known, the child was removed from the family and returned to Germany.[96] Another child was beaten so badly by his foster father that he had to spend three weeks in hospital. He was then sent to another family in Co. Clare, where he spent nine very happy years. He returned to his family in Germany in 1956 but could not settle down there, and came back to Ireland where has lived ever since.[97]

Home – Germany or Ireland?

In 1949 the Red Cross was faced with the question of how and when the first children were to return to Germany. It had originally been intended that they should stay for a maximum of three years, and this time was up in the spring of 1949 for the first arrivals.[98] In April 1949 two transports, the first containing forty-eight children, the second sixty, were organised.[99] Many children wanted to stay in Ireland, however, and in most cases their foster parents were prepared to keep them.[100] The children had become part of the families in which they lived. A number of them only spoke English – Germany had become a very far away country and it was no longer home to them. Enno Stephan commented on the issue:

There were certain problems in that the children, because Ireland did not have adoption at the time, did not become Irish citizens but remained Germans without being able to speak German.[101]

The Red Cross had to keep to the arrangement made, however, and this stated that the children should return after three years. A conflict arose between those who wanted to carry out the official arrangements and the families who wanted to keep the children. The first departures took place in an atmosphere of despair and sorrow. Mrs Clissmann witnessed the day's events and described them thus:

> It was heartbreaking, it really was heartbreaking. There were all the Irish families and the children, and the children were laden down with lovely warm clothes and bicycles and God knows what else, and the parents were crying. I remember one man, he was sitting there and he was crying, tears were rolling down his face and he was saying 'they shouldn't have done this to us, they shouldn't have done this to us'.[102]

Years later one of the children involved, Ursula Becker, described her return to Germany as follows:

> [The foster family] was nearly hysterical with grief . . . But my mum thought she would never see me again so I had to leave. That was very very awful for me, I cried all the way. Back in Germany the whole family were waiting . . . father, mother, older sister, a three year old sister I had never met, grandparents and an aunt. I had forgotten all my German, all I could say was 'hello, hello'.[103]

In February 1949 the Save the German Children Society started a campaign to get permission from the government for the children to stay in Ireland.[104] Oliver Flanagan TD wrote to the government in March 1949 that he hoped that the wishes of certain families to keep the children would be fulfilled.[105] He received the reply that the Minister for External Affairs had no objection in principle to the children staying:

> The Save the German Children Society . . . had consulted this Department [of External Affairs] and the Department of Justice who had informed them that so far as these Departments were concerned, no pressure was being put on any of these children to leave the country and that, provided that the consent of the parents or guardians in Germany was obtained, there would be no objection to their remaining on.[106]

In May a meeting between the Red Cross and the Department of External Affairs took place, during which the Red Cross representatives complained about the Save the German Children Society:

> The Save the German Children Society was making itself very busy in trying to secure an extension of their stay . . . [they] had been canvassing the foster-parents to keep the children and generally proving a nuisance to the Red Cross Society.[107]

The Department stated that the children could stay if the parents in Germany agreed to such a move. According to Werner Friedrichs, who researched the case in the 1970s, around fifty of the children were allowed to stay.[108] After the final Red Cross transport which took place in September 1949, the foster-parents alone were responsible for the remaining children.[109] Some children returned to Germany but could not settle and came back to Ireland.[110] In some cases, the child's mother came from Germany to take her son or daughter back, but agreed to leave the child in Ireland after seeing how well adapted he or she had become to Irish life.

Work for the Save the German Children Society did not end here. The organisation continued to collect clothing and food which it sent to Germany through the Irish Red Cross. After the Red Cross stopped this work in 1949, the Save the German Children Society continued alone.[111] From June 1948 the society also published a magazine called *The Bulletin*, which reported on conditions in Germany and on Irish aid. The magazine also contained articles which had distinct political tones. This is an example of an article published in July 1950:

> The bulwark of Christianity and the white race against the Huns, Tartars, Mongols, Mohammedans and Bolsheviks has been destroyed. 'Unconditional Surrender', born of a cruel heart, has bled Germany almost white. The world of misled people who have worked to create such terrible murder weapons as brought about this great catastrophe, must now work with a thousandfold greater determination for a lasting peace built, not on lies, hatred, revenge and greed, but on trust and justice . . .[112]

This article was not only racist, but it also placed the blame for the Second World War on the shoulders of those who created modern weapons. The guilt of the German people was not mentioned, rather the Allies were accused of causing widespread suffering. *The Bulletin* was also used to draw attention to Ireland's fate during British occupation. In the 'Kindergarten' section, for example, the children were told the story of Michael Davitt, after which it was stated: 'It all reads much like the sad stories one reads today about boys and girls in Germany – a land now suffering as Ireland did for over 700 years.'[113] These are examples of political opinions which were not shared by the majority of the members, but which were heard from time to time and which constantly damaged the Society's image in the eyes of the British authorities.

GERMAN GRATITUDE

The humanitarian work that was carried out by the Save the German Children Society outweighed by far the political incidents that sometimes overshadowed the Society. Its work was deeply appreciated by the children, the parents and foster-parents and also by the German authorities. In September 1950, the Society wrote to the Consulate General of the Federal Republic of Germany in London, asking whether aid was still required for Germany. The letter was forwarded to the Office for Foreign Affairs in Bonn which replied confirming that this was the case, and praising the Society's work:

> I should not fail to avail myself of this opportunity to convey to you the very sincere thanks of the Office for Foreign Affairs for the generous material help by which you have relieved the dire misery of many Germany children, and to assure you that this token of humane understanding will remain unforgotten by all those who witness the affliction of the homeless youths.[114]

In 1952 the German envoy to Ireland, Dr Katzenberger, held a reception for the Save the German Children Society. He presented them with gifts from the Caritas organisation and from the Protestant Aid Organisation (Evangelisches Hilfswerk) which were to be raffled for the Save the German Children Society. He spoke of the good work which had been done by the members:

> We all know what noble work the Save the German Children Society have done during the hard years after the War, and still do. They do not ask for thanks nor gratitude although they spend ['donate' is meant here] with full hands and literally saved thousands of German Children by feeding, housing, and clothing them. All this has been achieved on a strictly voluntary and private basis and by people who do not belong to the wealthiest on this earth.[115]

The gifts were accepted by the President of the Society, the Lord Mayor of Dublin, Senator Andrew Clarkin. He expressed his thanks for the gifts and mentioned the great famine which had struck Ireland the previous century, the memory of which was one of the reasons for the generous donations given by the Irish people to Germany.[116] In his report on this reception to his government, Katzenberger wrote that the Society would probably cease its activities the following year (1952).[117] There are no further details available in the files as to when the Society ceased to exist, but because it is not mentioned after the year 1951 it can be assumed that it was indeed dissolved in 1952.

The greatest success of the Save the German Children Society, and of those who personally contributed to the work, was first of all that they eased the lot and indeed saved the lives of many children. Secondly they contributed to humanitarian and democratic thought in post-war Europe, and thirdly that close ties were created between Irish and German families. All those who were involved in the work and who were questioned for this study still show lively interest in Germany. Some of them learnt German in order to be able to visit and learn about the country. Others still visit their former foster-children or foster-brothers and sisters, and send their own families on cultural trips to Germany.

One of the many fascinating stories about the contact between German and Irish people which began at this time is that of Herbert Remmel, who came to Ireland in the first group of children in 1946. He had two foster families – the Cunninghams in Dublin and the Nallys in Mayo. In 1949 he left Ireland because his parents in Germany wanted him back. He returned for a visit in 1956, but his next visit was only possible many years later, in 1990, since he lived in the German Democratic Republic and thus could not travel. The fact that he did return after so many years testifies to the strong links which survived a forty-year separation. Herbert Remmel was welcomed in Ireland in 1990 as a member of the family and as an old school friend in his former home town in Mayo.[118]

The aid which was given by Ireland in the form of donations was acknowledged by the German people in later years. After Germany had recovered from the worst of the post-war period, German officials started to consider how the German people could express their thanks for the help they had received from other nations.

On 27 November, 1951, the Dankspende des Deutschen Volkes (Gratitude Fund of the German People) was founded. Its aim was

... to approach the world, the anonymous world of innumerable people who helped us, thorough a fund which we will call the gratitude fund, in order to give a symbolic present, a symbolic gift, which will express the thanks of the German people.[119]

By the time the fund was dissolved in March 1957, DM 1,314,510 had been collected.[120] In December 1953, the German government honoured Irish men and women who had helped German refugees, orphans and children. The workers of the Red Cross were singled out for special thanks and medals were presented to them at a ceremony at the German legation.[121]

In 1954 the Gratitude Fund presented the Irish nation with a sculpture by the German artist Josef Wackerle. The Irish authorities decided that the sculpture, which was called the Nornenbrunnen, should be placed in St. Stephen's Green in the centre of Dublin in order to serve as a 'permanent reminder of the close and friendly relations between our two peoples.'[122] Theodor Heuss, the German president, wrote to Tomás O'Ceallaigh:

> The most generous gifts sent by the Irish people to Germany have not been forgotten ... May I ask your Excellency to accept the fountain by the sculptor Josef Wackerle as a modest attempt to convey the gratitude we feel deep in our hearts to the Irish people.[123]

Unveiling the statue on 28 January, 1956, Katzenberger made a speech in which he pointed out the importance of foreign aid in the democratisation process in Germany:

> ... the Irish people [was] ... in the forefront and contributed to the relief of suffering in Germany with all its strength and in true Christian spirit ... The donations received from foreign countries contributed to strengthening the awareness of practical Christianity in the German people after a time of the crassest materialism and to the fact that the German people regard themselves as being inseparable from the Christian west.[124]

The speeches were given in German and in Irish, which led one of the German guests present to observe that the Dubliners gathered did not understand the one or the other language![125] The ceremony received widespread coverage in the Irish press, a fact which reflected the relatively large public interest in Germany at the time.

The Irish Red Cross, the Save the German Children Society and Caritas Catholica also received smaller tokens of appreciation.[126] In all gifts were presented to seven organisations by Werner Stephan, Ministerial Director of the fund.[127]

THE CIRCLE CLOSES

The events of 1946–49 and beyond were never forgotten by the children and families involved, although some did lose touch during the years. Public memory, however, quickly forgot this chapter of German–Irish relations. In the last two years, interest in the almost forgotten story of the German children who came to Ireland many years ago has been revived. The German embassy in Dublin took an interest in the matter and together with the Irish Red Cross succeeded in tracing over 160 of the 'children', now, of course, in their fifties and sixties. The result of the successful search was a reunion of the children and their foster-families in Dublin on 23 and 24 March 1997, the first day of which was attended by the German President, Dr Roman Herzog. For the first time in fifty-one years, those people who had arrived in Ireland after the terrors of war, and found a home there, stood together again in St Patrick's Cathedral in Dublin, listening to the President, Mary Robinson, Dr Herzog and the Lutheran Pastor Reverend Paul-Gerhard Fritz praise the work of the Irish people and pray for peace today.

The most emotional part of the commemoration for the 'children' was their trip to Glencree – the place where most of them had spent their first weeks in Ireland, arriving undernourished, traumatised and speaking no English. Talking to several of the 'children', it became clear that Ireland had been a welcome refuge from the very beginning; not one person could remember being homesick or afraid of the future. The memories were all of green hills after having experienced nothing but ruins, plentiful food after years of hunger and strict but kind treatment by the Red Cross volunteers at Glencree.

During the day at Glencree, memories were exchanged, experiences compared, old friends found and many tears shed. The actual building in which the children had been housed could not be viewed from the inside since it is in a state of disrepair, but in the other buildings the Centre for Peace and Reconciliation provided an appropriate venue for the reunion. The author was told stories of the years in Ireland; of a little boy throwing coins into the water because he didn't know the concept of money; of another boy trying to buy sweets with a cheque, not realising that it had to be filled in first; of the excitement of making their first communion or confirmation in

Klaus Kramer making his First Communion.
(Photo courtesy of Klaus Kramer)

Ireland; of Klaus Kramer who kept coming back to Ireland and in the 1980s got a job teaching German through Irish; of Helmi Saidléar, née Putz, who met her future husband at the commemoration of the 1916 rising in 1966 and who speaks only Irish with him and her children. For one girl, Maria Trypczyk, one of three sisters who had been fostered in Ireland, the day was to hold something which she had never expected. Fifty years ago during a stay at Glencree waiting to be chosen by new foster-parents, she lost a gold chain. One of the Red Cross workers later found it, but could not get in touch with her to return it. Now, on 24 March 1997, having kept the chain for fifty years, she was able to return it to its owner.

While the reunion was held to commemorate past events, the future, especially that of the European Union, was also a topic often mentioned during the speeches. Dr Herzog, visiting the statue in St Stephen's Green which had been presented to the Irish people in 1954, spoke of the futility of war and emphasised the importance of Europe today, declaring that the relief effort for German children and the links that had arisen from it 'confirm my view that Europe is not only economically but also culturally and politically important'. At the reception which followed in Dublin Castle, Herzog declared:

> Operation Shamrock is a European symbol . . . There was no clash of identities, as today's Eurosceptics would forecast. Even then Europe had a human dimension . . . which builds bridges, even over language barriers.

The then Minister for Finance, Ruairi Quinn, in a speech made at a reception at Iveagh House, emphasised the importance of Europe today, saying:

> European Monetary Union has a value much stronger than its financial value. Those united by a single currency will never go to war with each other again.

The German and Irish families standing side by side were indeed a testimony to the importance of European links. While for the most part, the children's foster-parents had passed away or were too old to attend the ceremonies, the fact that the children were accompanied by their foster-brothers and sisters, cousins, nephews and nieces and friends of the family bore witness to the bonds which have been maintained into the next generation.

CHAPTER FOUR

Trade and diplomacy

THE RENEWAL 1946-50

When the war broke out, trade between Ireland and Germany became impossible. From 1946 onwards, the Irish government showed considerable interest in resuming relations as quickly as possible, and the beginnings of trade between the two countries was witnessed that year.

All economic relations with the western part of Germany were controlled by the Allied Joint Export/Import Agency (JEIA). In 1947, new conditions for trade with the American and British zones of Germany were published. The details of these conditions were published in the *Irish Trade Journal*,[1] so that any Irish companies who were interested in trading with Germany could have the most up-to-date information. The publications stated that permission for trade between Ireland and Germany had to be granted by the German Economic Minister, the Irish Department of Finance and the JEIA, thus making trade bureaucratically difficult in the beginning.

In 1946, Ireland exported goods, mainly potatoes and medicines, to the value of £24,000 to Germany. (Humanitarian aid for Germany is not included in this figure.) Ireland imported hops, iron and steel products and machines to the value of £105,000 from the western zones of Germany. In 1947, trade between the countries was much lower than in the previous year due to restrictions put in place by the Allies, with trade at a value of £18,000 in both imports and exports. In 1948, trade increased again, although the amounts were still low in comparison to the pre-war figures.

In 1949 economic relations between Ireland and Germany slowly returned to normal. In March of that year, two representatives of the Irish Department of Agriculture visited Frankfurt. This visit was organised by the American legation in Dublin.[2] The representatives visited the JEIA headquarters in order to hold unofficial talks on trade possibilities between Germany and Ireland. These talks were to serve as an introduction to official trade discussions that took place later in the year. By June 1949, a new trade agreement was being planned between the two countries in order to normalise economic relations. With trade increasing considerably in 1949, although no agreement had yet been signed, the Irish government officially took the decision on 17 January, 1950, that a trade attaché for Germany was necessary in order to encourage the links. Another reason for this was that Germany was by then allowed to initiate foreign relations and so diplomatic representation would soon be required in any case. The Irish government decided to name its representative 'General Consul' rather than 'Economic Consul' in order to provide him with a mandate to deal with ministers on a higher level, and not just with economic representatives:

> It is obviously desirable, for economy and other reasons, that the officer appointed – although he will normally be engaged almost whole-time on trade matters – should be in a position to handle also any official business arising between the Irish and Western German Governments, as well as consular matters arising in connection with Irish travellers or interests in Western Germany.[3]

In order to rebuild the contacts, which had been promising before the war, John Belton, the then head of the Trade Division of the Department of External Affairs and a fluent German speaker, was named as the representative.

In October 1950 the Irish government received a telegram from Belton, who was based in Frankfurt, to say that he had been informed by the French High Commissioner of Germany's wish to establish diplomatic relations with Ireland.[4] Belton reported Ludwig Erhard, the economic brain of the new German government, as saying that the planned consulate was to be raised to the status of a legation as soon as possible. He also said that Erhard had mentioned to him the kindness with which the former German representative, Dr Hempel, had been treated:

> In the course of a conversation last week with Professor Erhard, Minister for Economic Affairs, he was very enthusiastic about the idea of establishing a German Consulate-General in Dublin . . . He expressed the highest appreciation of the manner in which the Irish Government had at all times treated Dr Hempel and his staff, particularly after the war.[5]

De Valera's treatment of Hempel had obviously been favourably registered by the Bonn government.

The German consulate in Dublin was not opened until June 1951, since all German government papers had to be sent to Dublin via the Allies and vice versa. This procedure was time consuming and meant that although Ireland had a consulate in Germany from 1950, German representation could only be established in Ireland from mid-1951. In the time before the consulate was established in Dublin, Belton attempted to accelerate the bureaucratic process and to convince the German authorities of the importance of German–Irish relations for both countries. From the protocol of a meeting between Belton and a member of the German Foreign Office, Kordt, the anxiety of the Irish representative to promote relations between the countries, especially given the division of both Ireland and Germany as a perceived common denominator, becomes evident:

> The Federal Government could be assured [wrote Kordt of Belton's words] that the future German general consul in Dublin would be accepted with the great friendship which the Irish people had always felt for the German people. Ireland and the Federal Republic shared the same fate as regarded the history of their native countries. Neither would rest until unity had been restored.[6]

On 4 June, 1951, the establishment of direct diplomatic relations between Ireland and Germany in the form of legations was announced. Up until then, Belton had only had the position of consul; he now became an envoy. The German envoy to Ireland was Dr Hermann Katzenberger, who up until then had been Federal Administrative Consul and was one of the founding members of the ruling Christian Democratic Party (CDU). In handing over his accreditation to the German President, Belton emphasised the cultural and economic ties between the countries and praised the German reconstruction effort:

> The Irish people have watched with interest and admiration the wonderful economic recovery of the German nation since the end of the war. They have also welcomed the establishment of a German Foreign Office and the increasing participation of this great country in international affairs. They look forward to that participation being developed to the greatest extent possible.[7]

At his accreditation, Katzenberger emphasised the Irish culture and thanked the Irish people in Germany's name for their help after the war:

> I know that I speak in Germany's name when I express to Your
> Excellency and the Irish people the heartfelt thanks of the German
> people for their generous help for Germany after the war and the help
> which they are still giving to many German children. This assistance is
> especially valuable because Ireland itself had to save to be able to help.
> The country contributed to strengthening Germany in its resistance to
> communism.[8]

The reference to communism was particularly welcomed by Irish
officials, being one of the rare mentions of politics by a German
representative. The press was present at the opening of the German
legation in Dublin in 'surprisingly large numbers'[9], as Katzenberger
himself put it, and the event was commented on at length in all the
main newspapers. The century-long historic links between the two
countries, and the fact that Katzenberger was a Catholic, were the
main points mentioned. *The Standard*, for example, acclaimed him as
'the best that Catholic Germany could present'.[10] It was appropriate
that the Germans had chosen a Catholic to represent them in Ireland,
given the fact that religion pervaded almost all elements of society at
the time. The attention given to Katzenberger's appointment is a
testimony to the importance of relations with Germany and the
interest devoted to Germany in Ireland. In the following years,
mutual relations in the areas of the economy, culture and politics
were encouraged and strengthened by the diplomatic representatives.

TRADE EXPANSION

In 1949 Irish exports to Germany increased to the sum of £1.5
million. After John Belton had been appointed consul general to
Germany in 1950, work began on a trade agreement which was
signed in July 1950 and was adapted and renewed in the following
years. The agreement of 1950 declared that Ireland could export
goods to the value of £1,900,000 to Germany and could import to
the value of £2,250,000. In September 1950, the first personal
contacts took place, with nineteen Irish companies taking part in the
Frankfurt Trade Fair.

In 1951 the trade agreement was due to be renewed. The Irish
placed considerable emphasis on the successful conclusion of the
trade negotiations and sent for John Belton to come from Bonn to
Dublin in order to take part in the talks:

The Foreign Trade Committee takes the view, and indeed consider that it is virtually essential for the proper conduct of the negotiations by the Irish delegation, that a member of the Consulate General in Germany should be available in Dublin before the negotiations open in order to enable the delegation to obtain a first-hand account of the difficulties which have been experienced in operating the existing Agreement, the improvements which should consequently be sought in connection with next year's agreement, and the potentialities of Germany as a market for specific Irish products . . . Germany's economic position has . . . deteriorated gravely in recent months and if we are to maintain the position which we have won for Irish products in that market it is essential that the greatest care should be taken with the forthcoming negotiations.[11]

Belton, who arrived in Dublin shortly before the German delegation in order to meet with government members, pointed out that the Germans considered it important to the success of any negotiations to discuss the validity of the 1930 trade agreement. The German delegation, led by Dr van Scherpenberg, represented the view that this agreement was still valid, since the Federal Republic considered itself the legal successor to the 'Third Reich'.[12] In the end, Ireland recognised the validity of the 1930 agreement, but stated that the 1950 agreement should be renewed and should determine German–Irish economic relations.

For Ireland, trade with Germany was of great importance because the country could acquire raw materials and machines that were not available in Ireland. At the same time, the Irish government tried to use the relations with Germany to gain greater independence from the British market.

The main exports from Ireland to Germany were cattle, barley, feathers, wool and woollen products, cheese and yarn. Ireland imported fertilisers, machines, tools, raw steel, cars, photographic equipment, silk, surgical and laboratory equipment and electrical goods.[13]

The following table shows trade between Germany and Ireland before the war and up to 1955.[14]

IRISH TRADE WITH GERMANY

1938			
IMPORTS	1,479, 267		
EXPORTS	912,369		
RE-EXPORTS	8,777		

(up to 1945 with the German Reich)

	1945	1946	1947	1948
IMPORTS	7,003	105,393	18,638	171,362
EXPORTS	–	23,956	18,229	74,984
RE-EXPORTS	–	–	30	–

(from 1945 with the western zone)

	1949	1950	1951	1952
IMPORTS	455,108	1,915,249	4,572,921	5,390,624
EXPORTS	396,405	1,460,174	1,175,438	865,759
RE-EXPORTS	1,530	5,491	5,661	22,909

	1953	1954	1955	
IMPORTS	5,274,631	7,347,892	9,552,571	
EXPORTS	894,476	1,751,253	1,412,843	
RE-EXPORTS	22,180	36,512	44,733	

(from 1949 with the Federal Republic)

By 1952 the Irish government was convinced that trade with Germany should and would increase, and therefore ordered the construction of a permanent exhibition stand at the Frankfurt Trade Fair in order to facilitate Irish companies to make contacts in Germany. Tourist information about Ireland, which up until then had been very difficult to get in Germany, was also to be distributed there. The pavilion was opened on 31 August, 1952, by the Tánaiste and Minister for Industry and Commerce, Seán Lemass. Lemass used his visit to Germany to hold a meeting with Ludger Westrick, Secretary of State in the Department of Industry, and to visit Chancellor Adenauer, the Minister for Transport Seebohm and the Minister for Agriculture Niklas. In his speech at the opening of the pavilion, Lemass took the opportunity of drawing attention to the political situation in Ireland, as did most Irish politicians when speaking abroad. The speech was cited in an Irish government newspaper:

> . . . there was one political problem which we in Ireland had in common with the people of Germany, and that problem was of such importance that it affected every phase of our life, including our national economy. 'I refer, of course', said Mr Lemass, 'to the fact that our country, which is naturally one has been artificially divided . . . We knew in any case, as the people of Germany did in respect to their country, that national unity must one day be restored.'[15]

The partition issue was mentioned by Irish government representatives at every possible opportunity, although they could not hope to bring about significant changes in the situation by doing this (see Chapter Five). In this case Lemass was referring to the fact that the six northern counties historically formed the main industrial area of Ireland and that partition, therefore, had a negative effect on the Irish economy. Dr Katzenberger wrote a report for his superiors describing the coverage which Lemass' visit had received in Ireland and also mentioning that, in his opinion, the visit did not only have an economic but also a political background:

> The general impression is that both the Irish government and the Irish public welcome the extension of German–Irish trade because by this a small further step is being taken towards breaking away from English [economic] predominance.[16]

This was indeed one of the main aims of the Irish government regarding trade with Germany.

In Germany, Lemass' visit was widely covered by the press, although no newspaper mentioned the issue of partition – this attempt to gain attention in Germany for the problem failed. Economic issues were, however, reported on in a positive light. Much was written about the developing economic relations between Ireland and Germany:

> It has not been forgotten in Ireland that the first step of the young Free State to build up its industry and its hydro-power occurred with German help [1926–1929, when the Shannon Hydro-Electric Works were built by Siemens] . . . The good reputation of German products has not suffered from the war.[17]

The favourable business conditions in Ireland were also mentioned:

> In general German goods and companies have a good reputation in Ireland. The usual caution when making business contacts should not be neglected, but particular fears are not necessary, since the desire for honesty in trade dominates in Ireland . . . One must use the existing German sales possibilities cleverly by carefully developing old and making new business contacts with Irish companies.[18]

Such articles strengthened the good reputation of Irish businessmen in Germany. This was also mentioned in the *Leaflet for German Foreign Trade*, a publication which offered guidelines to business-people:

> The Irishman is as a rule an honest and dependable businessman. He expects the same honesty, punctuality and dependability from his partner. Cases of bankruptcy and embezzlement are rare.[19]

Ireland thus enjoyed the same esteem in the economic sphere as in that of cultural and diplomatic relations. It was here rather than in the political arena that German interest in, and liking for, Irish matters was advantageous to Ireland.

In spite of the annual agreements, the opening of the pavilion in Frankfurt and the positive press reports after Lemass's visit, exports from Ireland to Germany dropped considerably in the years 1952 and 1953. The reason for this was the limitation on the import of various products by the German government due to the difficulties being experienced by the German state in balancing its international trade deficit.[20] By 1954 this problem had largely been solved and trade increased again. The Irish government did not, however, succeed in reducing the imbalance in trade which existed to Ireland's disadvantage. In spite of an industrialisation programme, Irish industry was in a grave crisis at this time. The Irish government did not manage to make the country less dependent on Britain during the 1950s. In 1951, imports from Britain made up 45% of Irish trade, and exports to Britain 75%. Only 2.2% of all imports originated in Germany and 1.5% of exports from Ireland were to the latter country. In 1957, 52.5% of all imports came from Britain and 61% of Irish products ended up on the British market. In that year, 3.7% of the imports came from Germany and 2.5% of Irish exports were sold to the German market.[21] Although trade with Germany increased in the following years, the figures still remained very low in comparison with trade with Britain.

From the mid-1950s, the Irish government made a concerted effort to bring foreign capital into the country. In 1955 the Industrial Development Authority, which had been founded in 1950, sent a letter to German umbrella organisations responsible for various industries (e.g. medical products, synthetic goods, textile and tool production etc.), in order to interest their members in trade with Ireland, and in particular in establishing a branch in Ireland. The fact that Irish goods could be exported to England duty-free, that wages were relatively low and that Ireland had had a stable government for over thirty years was mentioned in the letter. There was considerable interest on behalf of some German companies in this offer. As a result of this interest, the Irish Minister for Industry and Commerce, Norton, travelled to Germany in August in order to further promote trade possibilities. He emphasised again the duty-free export of goods to England enjoyed by companies in Ireland. This fact was immediately attacked by the British press as an attempt to get German goods onto the English market to Ireland's advantage:

> Plans are being perfected in Dublin to bring into Britain by the back door German goods free from custom duty or liable to preferential treatment. The entire British Commonwealth will have to concern itself with this new threat.[22]

There was nothing, however, that the British government could do about this, since it was Ireland's right to attract foreign capital into the country and to allow the foreign investors to profit from the advantages of an Irish location. The German press gave substantial coverage to this possibility to export to England via Ireland and reported on it in some articles that were to prove useful to the scheme in spreading publicity.

The attempts to promote foreign trade with and in Ireland were continued in the course of the following years. In 1957 and 1958 tax benefits were introduced for foreign companies in Ireland. In 1959 the Shannon Free Airport Development Company was established in the West in order to benefit the area through foreign investments.[23] In 1956 an air traffic agreement was signed between Ireland and Germany which allowed flights between the countries and permitted each country to use the other as a stop-over destination.[24] From 1957 no visas were required for entry into the respective countries, a measure which simplified trade contacts. By 1965, thirty-six German companies, one of which was Faber-Castell, had established branches in Ireland. These companies produced many varied products, such as clothing, carpets and leather goods. The efforts made by the Irish government had had an effect, and trade with Germany increased annually. It was not until the 1970s, however, that trade with EEC countries took on a much greater significance for the Irish economy.

CHAPTER FIVE

Cultural relations

RELATIONS BEFORE 1945

In dealing with cultural relations between Germany and Ireland in the 1940s and 1950s, it is not the quantity of people involved in cultural affairs that was important, but the quality of work carried out in this field. Although the number of members in cultural organisations was relatively small, the contacts built up in these years were to develop and become very important in a continuing cultural exchange between the countries. Those who participated in German–Irish cultural relations could draw on a long tradition of cultural exchange. This had begun with Christian contacts, when Irish preachers travelled to Germany in the seventh century. Their scripts and the so-called 'Scottish Monasteries' which they left behind have provided scholars with considerable information about this period. This was one of the reasons for the interest of German scholars in Celtic matters – an interest which was very lively in the period being dealt with here. They were following in the footsteps of academics such as Kasper Zeuss, who established the links between the Celtic and the Indo-Germanic languages; Kuno Mcycr, who translated numerous Irish texts, and Rudolph Thurneysen, an expert in old Irish literature and law, who through his activities had awakened a strong interest in Germany in Celtic studies.

The first German department in Ireland or Britain was founded in 1776 at Trinity College Dublin. This university became very important for German–Irish cultural relations through a small number of enthusiastic scholars. Despite the involvement of some very dedicated people, however, knowledge in Ireland about Germany remained sparse until well into the twentieth century, whereas German cultural interest in Ireland was relatively well developed:

> In Germany however the small amount of knowledge about Ireland in the so-called educated bourgeoisie in the twentieth century was taken from good sources, and an Ireland-friendly tendency was passed on

from one generation to the next. In the Gaelic population of Ireland however an educated bourgeoisie which would have been able to interest itself in Germany through reading and journeys and to form a certain opinion on the people and culture was missing in the twentieth century.[1]

In the period being treated here, this situation began to change and German studies in Ireland occupied an increasingly important role.

The 'Irish Nazi'

In the field of cultural relations, the efforts of individual people to keep interest alive played a large role during and after the war. It was generally only in the 1950s that official German–Irish societies and organisations were founded. During and immediately after the war, one man to a large extent led German academic activities in Ireland, a man whose political leanings were, however, dubious – Dr Heinrich Becker.

Although the use of Irish steadily decreased during the twentieth century, German academic interest in the language and its roots remained strong. German academics often had a better knowledge of the Irish language than many Irish people. Dr Heinrich Becker had travelled to Ireland shortly before the outbreak of the Second World War to study the country and its language. After the war began and all exchange students were required to return to Germany, Dr Becker was suddenly missing in the west of Ireland. He managed to stay there for the duration of the war and for many years afterwards. In this time he learnt to speak perfect Irish. During the war, Becker earned money by giving German lessons – always under the watchful eye of the Irish secret service. He estimated the number of students in his courses at over three hundred per year, and beginners' classes with seventy students were not unusual. The groups were composed of very different sorts of people, from the 'eager tradesman to the secretary of state'.[2] The participants studied under adverse conditions, as Elisabeth Clissmann remembered:

> Friends of mine who used to go to his classes were full of admiration because in those days there was no fuel and so you sat in your overcoat and gloves and hat and everything.[3]

Becker also travelled throughout Ireland in this time and took photographs and drew sketches of the Irish countryside, which he exhibited in Bonn years later. It may seem strange in retrospect that a German citizen was allowed to travel through Ireland with a camera during the war, but G2 observation was so strict that Becker could not have sent any photos to Germany even if he had wanted to. The secret service was aware of the fact that Becker was a member of the NSDAP (National Sozialistische Deutsche Arbeiter Partei), and observed him very closely for this reason.[4] Becker later mocked the suspicions of the Irish police in a poem he wrote:

> . . . He [Becker himself] was under suspicion,
> that he was taking photos in Ireland,
> which he (it was said, he could),
> personally sent to Germany by sub.[5]

Becker often felt the scrutiny of the secret service during the war. In 1944 he wanted to hold an exhibition of his photography in Dublin. The German envoy, Dr Hempel, supported this plan in order, as he saw it, to promote the tradition of German interest in Celtic studies.[6] The Irish secret service, however, was not of the opinion that this was the right time for a German to hold an exhibition in Dublin. Colonel Byran advised the government against granting permission. It does seem rather strange that the government refused the exhibition but, on the other hand, had no objections to Becker giving German lessons, since these classes could have easily been used to spread propaganda. It can be surmised that the authorities allowed the lessons to go ahead so that they would know exactly where he was and what he was doing.

After the war Becker remained one of the main protagonists of German–Irish cultural cooperation, first in Ireland and later in Germany. In 1945 he became involved in the Save the German Children Society (see Chapter Three) and he gave German lessons to the foster-children who were in danger of forgetting their native language.

CULTURAL SOCIETIES

Irish-German societies

Once relations between Ireland and Germany had been normalised in the years after the war, those interested in building up contacts between the two peoples began to organise themselves into groups. The first Irish–German society was established on 29 October, 1950, in Dublin after several people who were interested and involved in Irish–German affairs called for such a move, Proinnsias O'Sullivan,

Dr Kathleen Lynch, Dr Kathleen Murphy, Dr Becker and Helmut Clissmann amongst others. Some of the staff of the German legation also took part in the founding meeting, and Dr Katzenberger and his wife became patrons of the society. In his opening speech O'Sullivan warned the members not to drag politics into the society:

> I should like to stress that any speakers who take part in the discussions later should avoid any reference to politics, internal or external. This is not to be a political society in any sense of the word. Its aim is to cultivate friendly relations between our two countries, and controversial matters have no place in our deliberations.[7]

Since many of the members were already involved in the Save the German Children Society, they were aware of the difficulties which could arise if the Irish–German Society was labelled as an organisation with political motives. The sole aim was to encourage cultural relations, nothing more. It should be pointed out here that while the British and Irish governments mistrusted the Save the German Children Society, the German government did not harbour such concerns. When Stan O'Brien, an active member of the Save the German Children Society, was nominated president of the Irish–German Society in 1954, the move was welcomed by Katzenberger:

> Mr O'Brien has been known to the legation as very German-friendly from the beginning; for his activities [in the Save the German Children Society] he was awarded the Order of the Federal Republic of Germany last year.[8]

In order to maintain a clean reputation with the Irish authorities, however, the Irish–German Society had to remain strictly non-political. In a telegram to mark the official founding, Chancellor Adenauer expressed the hope that cultural relations between Ireland and Germany would be deepened by the society:

> The ties which have bound the Irish and the German people in the framework of European families were always particularly close. May you succeed in strengthening and intensifying these ties, particularly by deepening the cultural and personal relations.[9]

It was on this cultural and personal level that relations between Ireland and Germany could be developed to the advantage of both peoples and, equally importantly, had a real chance of success. On a political level, it could not be expected that the attempts made by

Irish politicians to place Northern Ireland and the issue of partition in the spotlight of German interest would bear fruit. In the cultural sphere, a lot could be achieved in the areas of academic contacts, the arts, tourism and personal contacts. The Irish–German Society concentrated on these areas, and politics did not become an issue for the Society. (For information on propaganda through culture see pp. 87–97).

An Irish–German Society was also founded in Cork in 1951, and the trend continued with the establishment of a Society in Galway in 1955. The Societies did not receive any direct financial assistance from the German government, since the latter feared that such sponsoring would be seen as an attempt to influence the independence of the Societies.[10] Funds were, however, made available for individual projects, for example to enable the establishment of a German library in Dublin.[11] Money was also granted by the Cultural Department of the German Foreign Office in the form of anonymous donations by a 'friend' of the Society.[12] The organisation in Cork also received unofficial assistance from this source from 1953 onwards.[13]

Dr Katzenberger recognised the possibilities that such societies could offer in strengthening relations between the two peoples and he was very involved in assuring their success. He regularly made suggestions to the Foreign Office as to how cultural exchanges between Ireland and Germany could be encouraged. Katzenberger was able to secure grants for scholarships, book donations and a salary for Dr Becker in his position as German teacher.[14] In 1952 he was able to acquire rooms in a house in Dublin for the Society, which had grown to 500 members.[15] The German Cultural Department approved the amount of DM8,000 for this purpose.[16] This investment turned out to be of value, as Katzenberger's report shows:

> Irish-German Society: It has developed excellently. Its events are always a great success. Above all, the house has proved to have been worthwhile, it is however almost too small now. The German financial contribution is not in the least apparent.[17]

This apparent independence from any government support was very important to Katzenberger.

Enno Stephan, a German journalist who spent a lot of time in Ireland in these years, expressed his opinion of the Society's reputation among Dublin people:

> It was well-attended by the, how should I put it, the somewhat better people in Dublin. It was considered chic to attend a function at which Germans were present.[18]

German cultural events, in other words, had not lost any popularity due to the war. The activities of the Irish–German Society were multifarious – lectures were given on history and art; German lessons were held for children; trips to Germany were organised for Irish students; receptions were given for German guests (e.g. for the members of the German PEN club or for Bavarian pilgrims who were visiting holy sites in Ireland) and hikes and dances were organised for the entertainment of the members. The German lessons for children gave rise to the idea of founding a German school in Dublin. This idea was realised in 1957 when St Kilians, which still exists today, was founded.

German visitors, such as the pilgrims mentioned above, were welcomed by the Irish–German Society as cultural friends, and political issues were not addressed. Despite this, politics almost inevitably played a part when German guests visited Ireland. The participants of the PEN congress, which took place in Ireland in 1953, reported the following:

> Almost every day we delegates were flooded with leaflets in the post which sometimes were for but much more often against the well-known partition of the country.[19]

It was almost inevitable that a visit which was only of a cultural nature was seized upon as an opportunity to spread propaganda by opponents of partition. The Irish–German Society was not involved in any of this activity, however.

Both the Irish–German Society and the German legation valued the reputation of independence which the Society enjoyed. In the 1960s, a problem arose in this area which was to result in the closure of the Society. In 1961 the intention to found a German cultural institute in Dublin was announced. The German government announced that this institute was to take over a considerable amount of responsibility in the cultural field. The Irish–German Society was to have no say in the new institute, since the latter was to be run by the German government. The Germans suggested that a division of tasks should take place. The leaders of the Irish–German Society in Dublin were not happy with this suggestion and, when no compromise could be found between the opposing points of view, they voted to dissolve the Irish–German Society.[20] This decision, however, was only taken by ninety-two of the one thousand members at one meeting and did not necessarily reflect the wishes of the majority of the members. Nevertheless, this did not alter the facts and the Society was dissolved. Some years later, however, other Irish–German relations were founded which were able to coexist with the Goethe Institute without any problems.

German-Irish Societies

In Germany after the war, the first German–Irish Society was founded in Bonn in 1953. The state of North-Rhine Westphalia and, in particular, the town of Bonn became the centre of German–Irish activities in post-war Germany. The Irish legation was set up there; a lot of business contacts were established in the area; Bonn University was well known for Celtic Studies; the state had a regional representative for Ireland, Dr Bringmann, and the Minister for Education, Mrs Teusch, was regarded by the Irish legation as 'quite sympathetic to Ireland'[21]. There was no better location for a German–Irish Society. Its president, Dr Rudolf Hertz, was a professor for Celtic Philology at Bonn University and the Society worked closely with the Celtic Department of the University.[22]

In the course of the preparations for the establishment of the society, Dr Heinrich Becker, who had been living in Germany since 1952 as a secondary school teacher, was suggested as Secretary to the Society. John Belton decided that he should first ask for information from Ireland about Becker in order to make sure that he was suitable for the post. So, before allowing the legation to take up direct contact with Becker, he wrote to Seán Nunan of External Affairs. The latter asked some questions and was given a report written by Colonel Dan Bryan in 1947, which stated:

> Becker prior to and in the early days of the war was a Nazi of good standing and actually indulged in German propaganda . . . [but] Becker seems to have been under the personal influence of Herr Hempel . . . who restrained him and kept him quiet . . . Generally, I understand Becker was a man of little sense and no shrewdness who in the early stages of the war attracted a good deal of attention careering around on a motor cycle . . . As a member of the Sturm Abteilung, Becker belonged to the Nazi party from 6th July 1933 . . . Although subject to close supervision during the war years, there was never any evidence that Becker was directly connected with espionage or subversive activities.[23]

In spite of this information which pointed unambiguously to the fact that Becker had been a member of the SA (until this was dissolved in 1934) and a Nazi sympathiser, Nunan chose only to cite the last sentence of the report in his reply to Belton and thus rendered the judgement harmless. Nunan added: 'From what we recall of Becker here, we have the impression that he should make a most energetic and capable organiser for the kind of society in contemplation.'[24] In Irish politics personal opinions often count more than official reports, and this led in this case to the unfortunate fact that an Irish civil servant helped a former Nazi sympathiser to establish his career after the war. Thanks to the recommendation, Becker was able to participate in the work of the German–Irish Society, and he established a work-group for the Irish language and culture in 1954.[25]

DEEPENING RELATIONS

The societies whose aim it was to encourage cultural and personal contacts between Germany and Ireland were able to claim considerable success during the 1950s. Complementary to the work carried out by the Cultural Departments of the two governments, the societies developed contacts which deepened with the years and the growing importance of the idea of Europe. A few examples of this kind of cultural exchange will be presented here.

One of the most exciting musical events in Dublin in the 1950s were the visits of the Hamburg State Opera three times between 1950 and 1954. In order to make the first of these visits possible, funds were made available from the Cultural Relations Committee.[26] The costs of an art exhibition in Dublin in June 1954 entitled 'German Graphics in the twentieth century' were also carried by the com-mittee.[27] In 1954 an exhibition of Dr Becker's photographs and drawings was held in Bonn. It was visited by representatives of the German Foreign Office and the Irish legation and received consid-erable coverage in the press.[28] The following year there was an exhibition of Irish art during the Sauerland Culture Weeks.[29]

Student exchanges were also important in the development of academic contacts between Ireland and Germany. In the beginning there were more opportunities available for Irish students who wanted to study in Germany than vice-versa, since there were no official funds granted by the Irish government to sponsor foreign students.[30] In the period examined here, the only scholarship available from an Irish institution was one granted by Trinity College after 1952.[31] This did not, however, stop German students coming to Ireland privately in order to get to know the country. One example is that of a group of Bavarian schoolchildren who were members of the Bavarian Youth Ring who came to Ireland in 1951 with the organisational help of a friend in Ireland.[32] Other student exchanges were made possible as a result of the good relations between the two countries which had been forged immediately after the war. The University of Aachen for example set up a scholarship for an Irish student as:

> a token of our appreciation and gratitude for the kindness of the Irish people in sending a large gift of bacon for distribution among under nourished students.[33]

The return of some of the German children who had lived in Ireland as part of Operation Shamrock, and the visits paid by some of the Irish foster–families in Germany, were a sign of the lively personal contacts between the German and Irish people.

German research institutes also took an interest in the study of Celtic philology. In 1952, Dr Hans Hartman of Göttingen University received a scholarship from the German Research Association to finance a stay in Ireland. He was also helped by a book donation from the Irish government.

Sport was another means of encouraging contacts between the peoples. In 1951 an Irish–German sports competition took place in Dublin. An employee of the German legation in Dublin, Mr Achilles, reported to the German Foreign Office on the speech which he held at the event:

> My short English and German speech culminated in mentioning that we Germans who for years have been seen and treated abroad as war criminals and are still seen in this way by the majority – we Germans consider it as a great satisfaction and pleasure that it was the Irish people who melted this iciness around us and led to way in creating a path of international understanding among sport-loving youths.[34]

It was these cultural and personal relations between Irish and German people, and not so much political issues, which reflect the true picture of German–Irish relations in the first decade after the war. Despite this, however, the Irish government remained active in its attempts to have political questions, and especially partition, addressed in connection with Germany, and this issue is the subject of the next chapter.

CHAPTER SIX

Political relations

THE BACKGROUND

Political relations between Ireland and Germany were resumed after 1949. Up to this time, all matters concerning Germany, such as the consequences of the war for the German diplomats, internees and spies in Ireland and the renewal of trade relations or cultural exchanges, were handled by the Allies. In 1949, both countries became republics. In Germany the division of the country that had originally been agreed to as a temporary administrative and power-dividing measure by the Allies was cemented by the founding of the Federal Republic of Germany and the German Democratic Republic. Ireland, too, was unable to unite the whole country into the republic and was forced to accept in reality the loss of the six northern counties. Both states regarded the political situation of their countries as temporary; neither the Federal Republic nor Ireland was prepared to officially recognise the division of its territory.

In the years after 1949, Ireland often referred to the German situation in order to promote understanding in Germany and elsewhere for the Irish desire for unity. The Germans, too, made some effort to gain understanding in Ireland for the situation in their country, although this was not done nearly as energetically as vice-versa. This question of 'propaganda' that was carried out by both countries will be dealt with in this chapter.

In Ireland there was considerable interest in Germany and German matters, both among politicians and in cultural and economic circles. This interest was based on the cultural and political ties that had existed between the countries for many years and which did not diminish during the war. In Germany there was also a relatively high level of interest in Ireland, despite the essentially unimportant position that the country played on the world political stage. This interest tended, however, to be based on a romantic image of Ireland as an 'unspoiled' country rather than on political issues.

PARTITION/GDR – A SIMILAR PROBLEM?

Certain parallels exist between Ireland's position from 1937 and Germany's from 1949. In 1949 the German Basic Law was passed. It was thus named because it was not intended as the permanent constitution but as a temporary document which would be changed as soon as Germany was reunited. The Federal Republic of Germany refused to recognise the German Democratic Republic until the thaw of Ostpolitik set in during the 1970s, and refused to enter into diplomatic relations with countries which recognised the GDR. The Irish constitution, passed in 1937, displays a similar line of thought:

> The national territory consists of the whole island of Ireland, its islands and the territorial sea . . . *Pending the re-integration of the national territory* and without prejudice to the right of the Parliament and Government established by this Constitution to exercise jurisdiction over the whole of that territory, the laws enacted by that parliament shall have the like area and extent of application as the laws of Saorstát Eireann and the like extra-territorial effect.[1]

In other words, the Irish claim to govern the whole of Ireland was not, and still has not been, renounced. The division of Germany, like that of Ireland, was always regarded as temporary even though both divisions deepened with time. The fact that German unity was achieved in 1990 occurred as a result of international developments, especially those within the Soviet Union, the economic unviability of the GDR and the wish of the East German people to be free. An end to partition in Ireland is not in sight, even if some movement has been made with the start of the peace process in 1994.

Propaganda

Irish propaganda in Germany

Although the position in Ireland resembled that in Germany in some ways, as has been outlined above, there were fundamental differences in the situations surrounding the division of the countries. The fact that the Irish government refused to acknowledge the division of the country led it to seek support and recognition abroad for the injustice of the situation in Northern Ireland. Germany, on the other hand, never had to go about obtaining recognition for its situation since the country was the geographic centre of the Cold War and, as such, of world wide importance. Ireland could not hope that the world would devote to its problems the same attention as was given to the German question.

In spite of this, the Irish government tried to maintain the image of Ireland being in a similar situation to that of Germany:

> . . . it is an American aim that Germany should be free and united. It is very generous indeed of the American people to state an aim so clearly about a people who until recently were at war with them. We have never been at war with America, thank God, and we never will I hope. We do not ask America to fight for us as she may have to fight if she is to implement that aim in regard to Germany. But we do believe that we are entitled to have our attitude respected when we say that we are as much entitled to freedom and unity as is Germany, France, Belgium, England or the United States itself and that we are not going to be content with less.[2]

The problem of the division of Ireland was, and is, officially paramount for the Irish government. Although not much could be done practically to achieve the reintegration of the six northern counties, reality was never allowed to overshadow the dream of a united Ireland. Therefore a considerable amount of effort was invested in propaganda which spoke out against partition. Germany was one of the main targets of Irish propaganda, alongside Britain and the United States. German officials dealing with Ireland were frequently confronted with this issue. Dr Katzenberger, German envoy to Ireland from 1950, knew that many Irish people still saw Germany as an enemy of Britain and reported on this to his superiors in Bonn:

> It is true that the official Irish policy and the population of Ireland is of a thoroughly friendly opinion regarding Germany. It should not be forgotten, in my opinion, that this friendliness is encouraged in part through the fact that Irish politicians strongly emphasise the tensions between Germany and England . . . I do not mean to distract from the friendly attitude of the country to Germany when I say this. Alongside the political, cultural and economic solidarity with Germany this motive does however play a certain role in the relations.[3]

Propaganda through culture
In 1946 and 1947 there were very few cultural contacts between Ireland and Germany, as has been seen in Chapter Five. It was only from 1949, after the situation in Germany had improved somewhat, that suggestions for the renewal of cultural cooperation were made to the governments by various individuals.

There were several ways of carrying out propaganda. When German academics and authors requested assistance from the Irish government in researching or publishing their works on Ireland, this was almost always granted when the Irish officials felt that the publication in question could serve to disseminate knowledge about Ireland. In these cases, the literature that was sent from Ireland to assist in research always contained information about the division of the country:

> We believe also that German language propaganda should enjoy a fairly high priority at present in view of the evident revival and re-participation of Germany in world affairs and the relatively high perspectivity among Germans at present for our case.[4]

In Ireland, a Cultural Relations Committee was founded by the government in 1949 to promote cultural matters. After the 1940s, which had been a repressive period culturally, and the censorship of the war years, the period from 1948–51 was somewhat more inno-vative on a cultural level:

> The inter-party government [Fine Gael, Labour, National Labour, Clann na Talmhan and Clann na Poblachta, 1948–51] had its defects, but its general benevolence towards the cultural world was refreshing and was appreciated by the artistic community.[5]

This cultural committee played a large role in German–Irish relations, in that it financially sponsored cultural exchanges between the two countries. The latter years of the 1950s were, however, infamous for the strict censorship that choked the world of culture to a large extent.

It can be said of the Cultural Relations Committee that its aim regarding German–Irish relations was to support writers and artists in order to contribute to better understanding and better cooperation between the two countries. But it should also be mentioned that the committee had a political aim, namely to disseminate knowledge about Ireland abroad in order to make the political situation of the country better known and thus to gain more understanding of Ireland's position. This political point of view was always taken into account when dealing with cultural projects, and those proposals which the Committee felt could fulfil this aim were generally supported.

The case of a lecturer of the University of Erlangen, Dr Kurt Wittig, serves as an example of this. Towards the end of 1946 he had written to the Irish government requesting assistance in getting a manuscript of his, dealing with Irish literature from 1889 to 1939, published. He wrote to say that he wished to make Irish literature more available to German students. It wasn't until 1949, however, when the Cultural Relations Committee was founded, that interest was taken in Dr Wittig's request. The Committee was of the opinion that it would be beneficial to assist Dr Wittig, since he was seen as 'the most active of our propagandists in Germany'[6]. In order to promote knowledge of Ireland in Germany he was granted a donation of books for the university:

> This donation includes . . . books on modern Irish history and the question of partition . . . It is suggested that this selection of books together with the pamphlets on the partition question which have been supplied from the Legation should be sufficient to give a clear picture of the matters on which Dr Wittig wishes to lecture.[7]

The issue of partition predominated all aspects of Irish politics. Wittig also received films about Ireland which he showed at various events in his area.[8] John Belton, the Irish envoy to Germany, saw the chance to improve tourism by showing films about Ireland in Germany:

> There is, as you can well imagine, a very great interest in Ireland to be found in Germany. During the last year the number of Germans who travelled abroad as tourists, increased very greatly and everything possible should be done to channel as many of these tourists as possible to Ireland.[9]

The Irish authorities, on the other hand, saw film distribution as a political matter. In 1954 responsibility for distributing films about Ireland abroad was handed over from the Cultural Division to the Information Division.[10]

A further example of the links between culture and politics is the cooperation between Irish authorities and Dr Joachim Gerstenberger. He was a German author and photographer and published a book on Ireland in 1940. He approched the Irish authorities in 1949 with the request that they financially support him in his research for a new book to be entitled *Ireland –Yesterday – Today – Tomorrow*.[11] The assistance was granted for the following reason:

> Dr Gerstenberger is entirely sympathetic to our point of view and intends to include in his work, if he can carry it out, material on Partition which would follow in a compressed form the line taken in 'Ireland's Right to Unity' [a political leaflet] which we have given him.[12]

The money that was sent to Dr Gerstenberger came from a government committee, the 'All-party Committee on Partition', which was set up in February 1949 'to launch a root and branch onslaught on partition'.[13] Gerstenberger later wrote an article in German for the INA (Irish News Agency) entitled 'What is Partition?'.[14] The fact that his request was dealt with by the All Party Committee on Partition and not by the Cultural Relations Committee implies the importance of cultural issues in the distribution of knowledge on partition. A book about Ireland, written by a German, was seen by many Irish politicians as a chance not only to provide German readers with a picture of Irish life and culture, but as an opportunity to carry out propaganda:

> A proposal has been put before us here which I think opens up interesting possibilities for a useful type of Anti-Partition publicity in Germany as well as in Austria and Switzerland.[15]

In 1949, Professor Dr Anne Heiermeier founded an Irish–Celtic Department at the University of Würzburg. She pointed out to the government in Dublin the extent of the problems she was facing due to the loss of books and manuscripts during the war:

> it was not an easy matter to have the interest in Irish Language and Literature inflamed and carried on again after simply every Irish grammar or dictionary had been destroyed.[16]

Professor Heiermeier therefore requested support from Ireland and drew attention to the long tradition of Irish studies in Würzburg in order to back up her request:

> Würzburg is not only in more modern times strongly connected with Irish studies by the name of J. C. Zeuss, the father of Celtic philology and other Celtic Scholars, its relations to Ireland go back as far as to those early centuries when Würzburg sheltered the most famous Irish Missionaries, Monks and Scholars, such as St Kilian, St Totnan and St Kolonat.[17]

As a result of this, Professor Heiermeier received a delivery of literature, including books on Irish history and politics, from the Cultural Relations Committee. Bonn University, which also had a long history of Celtic studies, was granted a donation of books from the Cultural Relations Committee as well,[18] as was the American Institute of Munich University, where the lecturer, Dr Heinrich Stammler, was to use these 'in the publicity work on this country which he has been carrying out.'[19]

Another German writer, Peter Grubbe (alias Klaus Volkmann),[20] was also granted financial aid from Ireland for his book on Ireland. De Valera even wrote an introduction for it after Conor Cruise O'Brien, who was then involved in the news services, pointed out that the author compared the division of Germany with partition and was therefore of use:

> . . . he mentions the parallels between the German and the Irish situation and says that the fact that the two countries have been divided against their will will make for understanding between the Germans and ourselves. In a book which will probably have a wide circulation these statements are of definite value.[21]

The author himself wrote to O'Brien that the book was not intended to be political, but that it would be clear to everyone which side he was on.[22] When Grubbe visited Ireland in 1954, he was received by the Taoiseach and was given the use of a car by the Irish tourist board – two details which proved his importance as a propagandist in the eyes of his hosts. The Irish authorities responsible for the matter made a big effort to ensure that Grubbe would be given a positive image of the country, especially because he was the London correspondent of the *Frankfurter Allgemeine Zeitung*, a large German daily newspaper. He was seen as an important contact and his newspaper as a potential source of information on Ireland in Germany. Many German correspondents in London also wrote about Ireland, and a large number of their reports were written very much from the English point of view, a fact which obviously was not of advantage to a positive portrayal of Ireland. Any chance to change this was welcomed by the Irish authorities.

In 1957 Irish authorities sent copies of the book *The Indivisible Island* by Frank Gallagher[23] to the Minister Presidents of the West German states and also to twenty-six German newspapers and journals, in the hope that this would contribute to knowledge of Ireland. One copy was sent to a newspaper in East Berlin by mistake because the sender did not realise from the address that the paper was in the East. This publication, *Die deutsche Außenpolitik* (*German Foreign Policy*), used the opportunity to publish an article about Ireland. In it, Sinn Féin was praised for, in the author's opinion, strengthening trade unions in northern Ireland which were working in the spirit of Marx and Engels. The author also wrote:

> The division of Ireland and the struggle of the Irish people for the re-unification of the country are naturally understood by the German people . . . Comparatively little attention is given to the – often successful – actions of the workers in strikes and demonstrations in this work which is, of course, written mainly with the aim of proving the injustice of partition.[24]

It is true that the Irish government wanted as much attention as possible for the division of the country, but such publications were not welcome. Ireland was far too anti-Communist and, in spite of its refusal to join NATO, much too bound to the western world to want support from a source such as this.

The dpa (German Press Agency) report on the book *The Indivisible Island* was much more to the liking of the Irish government. In it, Irish partition was described as being the first of many in the twentieth century, to be followed by the division of Germany, Palestine, Korea and Indochina. The journalist, Hans-Wilhelm Lehmann, agreed with Gallagher that the British had drawn the border in Northern Ireland with 'talent and cunning slyness much to their own advantage.'[25] Lehmann emphasised how important it was that the Germans should know about this problem and recommended the book for this purpose. The Irish government could not have asked for a more effective review, because to spread knowledge about the division of Ireland abroad in order to gain more understanding for the Irish situation in international organisations was its target. Acknowledgements of receipt of the book were also received from such notable figures as Heinrich Böll, August Zinn (Minister–President of Hessen) and Peter Altmeier (Minister–President of Rhineland-Palatinate). August Zinn commented on the book:

> This book has found my special interest because Germany has to expect similar consequences following the national partition as your nation had. It is our common aim to gain re-unification of our two countries in a democratic way. We Germans therefore have the greatest understanding for the most important aim of your government's policy. I am convinced that your Government too will do everything possible which may assist in the re-unification of Germany.[26]

It was, however, rare that German politicians mentioned possible support for Ireland from their country.

Other propaganda

Even Germans who had not specifically expressed any interest in politics were provided with information on the political situation when in Ireland or when dealing with the country in some way. Germans who made a stopover in Shannon, for example were given leaflets on the question of partition:

> His [one of the leading editors in West Germany] knowledge of partition was gained from an hour's stopdown in Shannon Airport, where he was given a pamphlet about partition which he read on the journey.[27]

Questions of an economic nature were answered with additional information of a political nature. For example, the Irish stand at the Frankfurt trade fair received copies of *Ireland's Right to Unity* in German as well as economic details for distribution.[28] This leaflet argued Ireland's right to the entire island of Ireland, using the example of the American civil war to emphasise the fact that 'only the nation in its entirety can have the right to self-determination'.[29] The government frequently tried to raise sympathy for the Irish question in Germany by using such well-known historical examples. In April 1951, the proposed German envoy to Ireland, Dr Katzenberger, visited his Irish counterpart, Belton, in Bonn in order to introduce himself and to get some information about Ireland. Belton gave him all the literature he had available and 'of course, a complete set of anti-partition literature.'[30]

Results of the propaganda activities

These efforts by the Irish government to spread knowledge about Ireland in Germany showed some success. However, this was more or less confined to the areas of culture and tourism. The German people reacted to the books and reports about Ireland in the newspapers in that they became interested in the country as a holiday destination. The 1960s were the decade in which German tourists discovered Ireland, not least thanks to Heinrich Böll's *Irisches Tagebuch*, which did more to interest Germans in Ireland than any amount of government literature. Many of them travelled there on holidays, and some stayed for ever. The interest in Ireland which had been interrupted by the war also reawakened on an academic level and Celtic Studies in Germany were supported by a small but enthusiastic group of people (see Chapter Five). This was an area where government assistance was of significant value.

Politically the influence of Irish propaganda was limited. There was considerable understanding among German politicians of Irish matters, but statements on partition were rare. Germany had to consider its position in relation to Britain; too much interest in the Irish problem would have marred these relations. For Katzenberger this meant that he had to exercise caution in the way in which he expressed himself in official circles in Dublin: he could not say too much on the issue of partition. Katzenberger therefore worked to keep relations between the two countries on an economic, cultural and tourist level instead of getting too involved in politics. In one of his first reports to his superiors in the Foreign Office, he explained the problem thus:

> The main question in Irish–English tensions, which can be regarded as permanent, is for us in how far we can strain our relations with England by taking an interest in the Irish way of thinking. In connection with this I must say – with every respect for the Irish friendship with Germany, which is certainly not only based on the negative influence of enmity with Britain, but also on true liking, economic and cultural links – that Ireland can only be evaluated as a second-level factor as regards political and economic weight in world politics. We must therefore be very careful in our actions. It would certainly be of no harm to show complete understanding for the problem of partition, not least because of our own position which has been created by the 'Iron Curtain'. Any more would however be unfavourably noted in England without us actually being able to help the Irish.[31]

This was a clear definition of Germany's position and a realistic one. No amount of propaganda could move Ireland into centre stage in world politics.

Information on Germany in Ireland
As has been seen, active efforts were made to spread propaganda about Irish affairs in Germany by various means. German interest in distributing information in Ireland was much more muted and, where efforts were made, considerably more discreet. Invitations to foreign journalists to visit Germany was one means used to provide information about conditions in the country and such visits were encouraged by the German government. In 1952, Dr Katzenberger, the German envoy to Ireland, suggested that some Irish journalists should travel to Germany in order to form their own personal opinions of the country. Katzenberger intended that the journalists should deal especially with 'questions involving travel and tourism.'[32]

He was a practical man and knew that Ireland and Germany were not of great importance for each other politically. He saw the possibility to promote relations between the countries on a cultural and tourist level (see also Chapter Five). The Foreign Office in Bonn, however, would only agree to finance the trip if the journalists were 'invited to a general, in particular a political orientation visit'.[33] Katzenberger thus had to organise a journey on this basis.

The Foreign Office approved a suggestion made by Katzenberger to invite the journalists individually instead of in a group. Katzenberger gave his reasons for this suggestion by explaining that Irish journalists were very individualistic and that there was heated rivalry between the newspapers. He further clarified this view, saying:

> we must, when dealing with the Irish, who like all natives of small countries are particularly independent and sometimes distrustful, exercise caution.[34]

Katzenberger may have overestimated the independent spirit of Irish journalists somewhat, but it is nevertheless true to say that the country's major newspapers were highly competitive amongst themselves.

The invitations to journalists from the *Irish Times*, the *Irish Press* and the *Irish Independent* were presented in July 1952. Kees van Hoek, the *Irish Times* corespondent, had to postpone the invitation until 1953 since he had already planned his own trip to Germany for 1952. In August 1952, Mr O'Donovan from the *Irish Independent* accepted the invitation and travelled to Germany, where he visited Bonn and Frankfurt and was informed in particular about tourism, German rearmament, the expellees from the east, the island of Helgoland (which was British-ruled for a time), and economic questions.[35] In September 1954, Peadar O'Curry, chief editor of the weekly paper *The Standard*, an expressly Catholic newspaper, also accepted an invitation from the Press and Information Department to travel to Germany. He was particularly interested in family and church matters. In August 1955 a further three Irish journalists travelled to Germany where they met, among others, the Foreign Minister Dr von Brentano, and Dr Middelmann from the Ministry for Refugees.[36] Thomas Kiernan, the new Irish envoy in Bonn, visited Berlin with the Irish journalists.

In 1954 Conor Cruise O'Brien, head of press information in External Affairs, was invited to Germany. The German Press and Information Department had decided to put up the funds for the trip considering 'his open-mindedness on German problems of which we are very aware.'[37] O'Brien visited Bonn, Mainz, Heidelberg, München, Berlin (including East Berlin) and Hamburg and wrote a report about his trip for the Irish government. He wrote about the Press and Information Department that Germany was not very concerned with propaganda: 'Other countries, notably Britain and America, make a far greater effort of propaganda than does Federal Germany'.[38] He continued with the comment that, in this opinion, the Department had a different task: 'I do not know of any Government which goes to such pains to keep itself supplied with full and up to the minute information. It is a listening post'.

On relations with Ireland, O'Brien wrote that Germany was far too occupied with its own problems to concern itself politically with a small country such as Ireland. As long as Germany was preparing its way to western integration, it would not afford Ireland any assistance regarding partition, he noted. Conor Cruise O'Brien was one of the few Irish authorities who realistically judged relations between Ireland and Germany. Furthermore, he was of the opinion that help from Germany would not lead to any significant moves towards ending partition. He saw future relations on other, more concrete levels, such as that of tourism. Germans were interested in Ireland, he stated, especially because they were so welcome there. It was, however, almost impossible to obtain information about Ireland in Germany. This was something which would have to be changed as soon as possible, he suggested. The Press and Information Department of the Federal Republic was satisfied with the journalists' visits to Ireland, since these resulted in many articles being published about Germany. It was noted that:

> as far as we can observe, neither the impression of [the trips] being a propaganda measure nor of showing preference to any particular newspaper has arisen.[39]

An effort was also made to inform the Irish public about Germany through the distribution of leaflets. The Cultural Attaché of the German legation in Dublin, Dr Kolb, complained that he did not know what to do with all the leaflets that he received from Germany. He was advised to distribute them to journalists, economic institutes and libraries. An effort was also made to distribute information on the fate of the expelled peoples from the former German territories. Von Richthofen, the Federal Cultural Consultant of the Land-mannschaft Schlesien (Silesian National Guard), who visited Ireland in 1953, observed after his visit that Germany should make more of an effort to publish information about itself in English.[40] He wanted the Foreign Office in Bonn to cooperate in particular with organisations such as the Kulturstelle der Landmannschaft Schlesien (Cultural Office of the Silesian National Guard) and the Sudetendeutschen-Tschechischen Föderativausschuß (Sudeten-German-Czech Federal Committee) which represented the views of expellees from the former Eastern provinces, in putting together information which was to be sent to German representative institutions abroad.

THE PRESS

Background – the German and Irish press

The German press
After the war numerous newspapers appeared in Germany – in 1948 there were fifty-six licensed publications in the American zone alone.[41] The press was extremely diverse, with large national as well as many regional papers. In the years immediately after the war, not many articles were published on Ireland, however, there being topics of worldwide importance that were more newsworthy. As well as this, German journalists did not have many opportunities to travel abroad to research feature stories due to visa and currency restrictions. From 1949 the number of articles on Ireland increased, especially since the Republic was founded in that year. In the early 1950s, relatively large numbers of articles were published about Ireland as a holiday destination. While Irish politics was not of great interest to German readers, the German press showed considerable general curiosity about the country. Brian Durnin, an employee of the Irish legation, commented that due to paper shortages, German newspapers usually only consisted of eight pages, of which only three were devoted to international events. Despite this, Ireland was written about relatively often.[42]

Those articles which did appear in Germany about Irish politics frequently concentrated on one or all of three issues: partition, economic problems and emigration. Of the bigger newspapers, *Die Zeit*, one of the most prestigious weekly papers, wrote about Ireland on a regular basis. The articles were well researched and generally lacking in any of the typical prejudices evident in other papers. As well as articles on Irish elections, this paper often published travel reports in which Irish friendliness towards Germans was particularly emphasised.

The Irish press

The press in Ireland was extremely provincial at this time. In spite of the major world events occurring, foreign news was only a small feature in most newspapers. Ireland devoted itself to domestic problems; only from 1955 did a real change occur. The country's voluntary isolation during the war continued well into the 1950s, and the press reflected this fact. Those articles on foreign affairs which were published were taken mostly from foreign press agencies or newspapers, since Irish newspapers could not afford to keep many correspondents abroad.

The biggest national newspapers were the *Irish Times*, the *Irish Independent* and the *Irish Press*. The *Irish Times* was seen as a pro-British paper and was the one which had been the most affected by censorship during the war. This newspaper contained the largest amount of international coverage. The *Irish Press* had been founded in 1931 by de Valera and represented the views of the Fianna Fáil party. It was:

> de Valera's newspaper . . . which, interacting with the efforts of Fianna Fáil and the overall economic and political situation, was the catalytic factor in bringing him into power (in 1932) which he held for sixteen years uninterruptedly and for a half a dozen years, intermittently, thereafter.[43]

The *Irish Independent* was this paper's main rival.

These three newspapers were described by an employee of the German legation as following:

> *Irish Times*, conservative paper with pro-British and Protestant leanings, small circulation; *Irish Press*, government paper, large circulation with supplements, and *Irish Independent*, liberal mass newspaper with supplements.[44]

As well as these papers there was a large number of small, regional newspapers, some of which occasionally published articles on Germany.

An examination of the Irish press in the years 1945–55 shows that articles about Germany appeared more often than those about other foreign countries. According to one estimation '[in the] Irish Times in the fifties . . . articles on Germany outweighed those on other European countries for many years in the ratio of three to two.'[45] The interest in Germany which had built up on a cultural and political level for many years did not fade during and after the war but rather was strengthened. Considerable attention was paid to the division of Germany and the reconstruction of West Germany.

The Irish news system changed after de Valera and Fianna Fáil lost power in 1948. A coalition government was formed by five parties, the most important of which were Fine Gael, Labour and Clann na Poblachta. This government, on the suggestion of Seán Mac Bride, established a news service – the Irish News Agency (INA) – in order to encourage the publication of Irish news abroad: 'Ireland's best wishes were not protected by a hostile international press and news agency system'.[46] The agency's aim was described thus:

> to disseminate Irish news throughout the world in order that the Irish viewpoint may get much more publicity than has hitherto been possible through the medium of the existing news agencies.[47]

Conor Cruise O'Brien was appointed head of the agency.

It is true that the foreign press, and especially the British press, published articles about Ireland that had an unfriendly tone or consisted of blatant untruths. A small number of such articles also appeared in Germany, most of which were written by British correspondents. The Irish agency, however, was never regarded as independent since it had been introduced directly by the government with the declared aim of spreading selected news about Ireland. The agency was closed in 1951 when Fianna Fáil regained power, and the Department of External Affairs took over its tasks.[48] The INA was very active during its short existence, however, and distribution of information from Ireland to foreign countries continued along these lines after its closure.

Irish perceptions of Germany

Several newspaper articles have already been analysed in the chapters on spies and on humanitarian work in this study. Almost all of these articles point to a very positive Irish image of Germany. Some more articles will be examined here, including articles about Germany in general and not only about German affairs affecting Ireland.

The German envoy in Ireland, Dr Katzenberger, regularly sent reports to Germany in which he analysed the Irish press in regard to Germany. He almost always reported that the articles showed very positive attitudes towards Germany: 'All of our large problems are followed with understanding and sympathy by the press and the public.'[49]

The division of Germany and the situation in the Soviet zone were widely covered by the press. All of the articles published in Ireland on this question displayed vehement anti-Communism – the influence of the Church rendered the appeal of Communism more or less powerless in Ireland. Headlines such as 'The Spirit of Freedom pitted against Soviet Tanks'[50] after the uprising of 17 June, 1953, were typical. Considerable attention also was paid to the Saar issue in 1954 and 1955, when the future of the area as a French or a German province was discussed.

The invitations to Irish journalists to visit Germany in the years from 1951 onwards led to a number of articles about the Federal Republic appearing in Irish newspapers, all of which were written in a way that reflected positively on Germany. In 1955, Kees van Hoek of the *Irish Times* wrote about the courage and the diligence of the Germans during the reconstruction of their country. He emphasised that, in his opinion, Germany should begin to concentrate on bringing about reunification, since the economy had started to recover and people could therefore concentrate on politics more.[51] This was a favourite topic among Irish journalists. Van Hoek also wrote an article about Adenauer which appeared in July 1952.[52] Katzenberger commented to his superiors about the article:

> For as long as I have been observing the Irish press, no article has appeared about a foreign statesman which was written in such a respectful and friendly tone as this one.[53]

Van Hoek emphasised the Catholic influences which had an effect on Adenauer and which, in his opinion, made the Chancellor even more appealing to the Irish people. In another article he wrote about the former German provinces in the east as 'the third Germany' (alongside the FRG and the GDR). Van Hoek supported the policy of non-recognition carried out by the FRG towards the GDR. Whenever he mentioned the GDR, he put the country in inverted commas, and he declared that the Bonn government was 'the only truly German mouthpiece, recognised by all the free and civilised world'.[54] (His interest in the territories east of the Oder and Neiße can be partially explained by the fact that his wife came from Danzig.)

Several articles also appeared in the *Irish Independent* after its journalist visited Germany in 1955. These concentrated on religious matters, the question of reunification and on Adenauer's work.[55] Irish interest in religion was reflected in articles such as that entitled 'How

West Germans Use Their Religious Freedom.'[56] The correspondent attacked the system in the East: 'The persecution with which the Church has to contend is not of the open and physical kind but is of a diabolical subtle and invisible nature'. Articles describing the suppression of the church in East Germany were common in the press in the 1950s.

The *Irish Independent* reporter published a large number of articles about the division of Germany in which he described the desire in East Germany and among the people from the Eastern provinces to become part of a united Germany: 'What they demand is nothing less than the Germany that was theirs before 1939, and this embraces the Saar, the territories east of the Oder-Neisse line now annexed by Poland and part by Russia.'[57] His sympathy for these people does not, however, take into account the reasons for the loss of the territories.

A lot of attention was paid to the Saarland issue in the 1950s, especially because many Irish people saw clear parallels between the situation in the Saar and that in Northern Ireland. In 1952, the issue of abuses of human rights in the Saar was raised by Germany at a European level. The Irish envoy to Bonn, Dr Belton, reported that Professor Hallstein, Adenauer's close advisor, had shown considerable interest in his questions on the matter and had expressed his hope that the matter would have the support of the Irish delegation in the European Council. Belton, pledging Irish interest in the matter, answered that 'Partition and the denial of human rights are a matter of the greatest interest and concern to us at all times'.[58]

From such newspaper articles it is evident that the Irish people had a lively interest in Germany and its fate. The articles analyse the division of the country, the economic recovery in West Germany and Adenauer's leadership, while strongly condemning the East German system. Such articles helped to considerably deepen the knowledge that Irish people had of Germany.

Politics and the 'romantic island' – German perceptions of Ireland

Quite a large amount of information about Ireland reached German journalists via the INA or the information division of the Department of External Affairs. Irish envoys in Bonn also made an effort to distribute Irish news in Germany and reported to the government on articles that appeared in Germany about Ireland. John Belton, Irish envoy from 1950 to 1955, sent the Minister for External Affairs an article from Germany that appeared in November 1950, in which the village of Pettigo, a small village which had been divided by the border to Northern Ireland, was described as Ireland's Berlin.[59] He commented on this:

> It is, of course, obvious, that no country in Europe can appreciate the evils of partition better than the Germany of today. It is my consistent experience that it is pushing an open door to explain to Germany how Irish people feel about the partition of Ireland. This, in my opinion, should not mean that we should not do everything possible to put our propaganda across here. There is a great deal of sympathy in this country for Ireland, because of our neutrality during the war and of partition. This sympathy should be developed and availed of to the full.[60]

Thomas Kiernan, Irish envoy from 1955, also made a big effort to have more articles published about Ireland and above all *by* Irish journalists. In order to avoid reports on Ireland always bring drawn from Reuters, Kiernan tried to persuade Dr Reinhardt, the Bonn representative of the German Press Agency (dpa), of the advantages of having a correspondent in Ireland. The dpa did not, however, act on the suggestion for financial reasons.[61]

Visits by German citizens to Ireland were another means by which information could be spread in Germany. In 1953, the Federal Cultural Advisor of the National Silesian Guard, von Richthofen, travelled to Ireland (see p. 97). He described his visit in a report to the German Foreign Office and dealt in detail with the foreign affairs issues which Ireland considered important. This report serves as a good example of the impression a German had of Ireland at this time. Von Richthofen had been invited to Dublin by the Irish–German Society to give a series of lectures.[62] The topic was Poetry as a bridge between the peoples. Their content was not only cultural and academic, as the title suggests, but political issues were also discussed. After a lecture on Russian, Polish, Czech and Ukrainian poetry, a discussion took place on the subject of 'displacement imperialism' and 'bolshevist terrorism'. During a lecture on 'The Celts in the prehistory of Eastern Germany' the terms East Germany and displacement imperialism were also discussed.

Many important representatives of Irish–German institutions were present at the lectures, including Dr Katzenberger and other members of the German legation staff, and Dr O'Sullivan, ministerial director of the Irish Ministry for Culture and member of the board of directors of the Irish–German Society.

Von Richthofen praised the efforts being made by the German legation to, 'continue to care for and favourably develop the old, enthusiastic Irish–German relations'. He emphasised that, in his opinion, it was not easy to be an official envoy in Ireland because of the 'strongly backward direction of many aspects of Irish political and economic life' and the 'emphatic anti-English attitude'. As did every other German visitor, von Richthofen only experienced positive attitudes to Germany. The Irish attitude towards England, however, was very different, he noted. This was so disapproving and distrustful that German guests sometimes found themselves in a difficult position because of it. He himself, he wrote, had tried to avoid this by drawing attention to 'the bolshevist danger which is the same for all of us'.

Von Richthofen then addressed the question with which every foreign guest was confronted: partition. This was the central issue of the entire policy of the Free State, he wrote. He stated that in this context Ireland was extremely anti-Communist, but that there was a strongly neutral leaning towards the Soviet Union because of the attitude towards Britain. On the subject of international relations, he noted that there was a marked isolationist atmosphere and that the idea of Ireland supporting a third power outside the Soviet Union or American field of influence received widespread support. He had observed a certain anti-American and, of course, anti-British atmosphere and had been warned that the Federal Republic should not let itself be 'tensioned between the wheels of the large self-assured western powers'. Von Richthofen reported that he had replied to such comments by again emphasising the worldwide Bolshevist threat.

He criticised the security measures in Ireland and the fact that the country was not prepared to increase its armed power. He saw the reason for this in the fact that Ireland was 'unable to see past old political relations' i.e. enmity with Britain – and that the country did not appreciate the dangers of Bolshevism.

He also criticised the gradual extinction of the Irish language, which he considered important in strengthening and preserving a national consciousness, and concluded that state incentives were not being carried out effectively or developed sufficiently.

He mentioned the personal contacts that he had made, among others Dr Scheyer of Trinity College who had been a lawyer in Silesia before fleeing to Ireland as a refugee from racism, and Professor Williams of University College Dublin, who had 'full understanding for our right to the German territories in the East'. This kind of comment pleased von Richthofen. He hoped through his visit to win

further understanding in Ireland of the aims of the expellee organisations in Germany. A German visit such as this, with an explicit
political undertone, was, however, rare. Generally official German
sources did not attempt to engage in overt political propaganda. Indeed,
the general German perception of Ireland, even among officials, was
a romanticised one, as will be seen below.

The majority of the articles which were published about Ireland in
Germany reflected the friendly attitude of most Germans towards the
Irish. The political problems of the country, its poetic beauty and the
friendliness of the inhabitants were themes which were frequently
addressed, with much more emphasis being placed on the latter two
aspects. The efforts made by the Irish government to draw attention
to the problem of partition did, however, bear some fruit. In 1954 an
article was published in the *Lichtenfelser Tageblatt* which offers a
good example of the kind of reports the Irish information authorities
wanted to promote. In the article, the partition of Ireland was
compared with that of Germany and other countries:

> These days there are some parts of the earth which have such political
> borders that divide peoples, one only has to think of Germany, Korea,
> Indochina. Today we can perhaps better understand the feelings of the
> Irish when they believe that they cannot accept the division of the
> border.[63]

As was so often the case in articles about Ireland, the journalist also
wrote about his reception in Ireland and how friendly this was:
'You're German? It's nice to see you here in Ireland! You know,
Germany has a lot of friends in our country!' He also described the
lifestyle and politics in Ireland, dedicating considerable attention to
the efforts to revive Irish as a spoken language. He offered his opinion
that Irish would never again become the native language – this was
the general conception expressed in the German press and it was an
accurate one. In the *Mannheimer Morgen* newspaper this question
was also dealt with in an entire article: 'A native language hardly
spoken'.[64] This reporter too did not disguise the fact that Irish would
never again be the spoken language in the country. This was not a
disadvantage, he claimed, because the Irish could avail of the 'cultural
and economic links to the world-wide English-speaking areas.'
Sympathy in Germany for Irish problems did not extend to understanding the efforts to reintroduce Irish as the main language.

In the German press many articles appeared which described
Ireland with such headlines as 'The island at the edge of time'[65] or

'The island between Pope and crown'. These articles were influenced by the traditional image of Ireland as a land of saints and scholars. The countryside, the friendliness of the people and the simple life were praised: 'The Irishman is good-tempered, very nationalist, dreamy and melancholy'. Juxtaposed with this was the other aspect of Irish life as perceived by many columnists – the 'fighting nature' of the Irish. The fight for independence through the years was often a topic in articles about Ireland, and some of these presented good historic knowledge. Often, however, the Irish 'fighting nature' was stereotyped and portrayed as belonging to the wild, whiskey drinking typical island man. In general it can be said that many of the articles on Ireland, which on the whole were positive, did still present the country as somewhat backward and that the German image of Ireland was often romanticised.

Articles on travel in German newspapers also often had Ireland as a topic. A report in *Die Zeit* in 1948 is a good example of this. In the article the author wrote about his friendly reception at Dublin airport: 'You're from Germany? Welcome in Ireland! You can tell that you're German. Because you're so thin'.[66] In the international climate of 1948 this warmth was unknown to Germans. And it was not only positive. When one Irishman said to the reporter that Germany had given the world a brave fight but that they had made one mistake in not going straight to Dunkirk in 1940, the latter had to object. In his article he wrote:

> . . . their love for Germany his without criticism and their admiration without differentiation. This friendship, this love, it does do you good when you are only used to being scorned. But it is also painful. I try, as carefully as I can, to say what I have to say about Germany and its fate.

The travel report that brought Ireland very close to German readers and which led to a considerable rise in tourism was Heinrich Böll's *Irisches Tagebuch*, which was published in 1957. The book can be seen as a declaration of love for Ireland and a contrast to the lifestyle in Germany, which Böll did not approve of. Böll first went to Ireland in 1954. He later wrote about this period:

> it almost looks as if we had caught Ireland in 1954 and 1955 in that historic moment when it had just begun to skip one and a half centuries and to be caught up by five others.[67]

Böll is describing the change in Irish society which was taking place at the time towards a more open and more European society.

Böll also noticed, however, that some Irish people showed a liking for Germany which indicated that they had ignored the realities of the events of the past years. He thus described himself as a 'travelling political dentist', who had to pull this political tooth no matter how much it hurt. The following describes one such scene:

> 'Tell me', he [an acquaintance] said quietly, 'Hitler wasn't – I don't think – such a bad man, he only went – I think – a little too far.'
>
> 'Listen to me, Pádraic,' I [Böll] said in a friendly tone, 'we know just how far Hitler went, he went over the bodies of several million Jews, children . . .'
>
> Pádraic's face twitched in pain . . . 'Pity, that you've let yourself be taken in by English propaganda, pity.'
>
> . . . 'Come on', I said, 'have the tooth taken out; it might hurt a bit, but it has to be done.'[68]

In the end Böll managed to convince Pádraic that he was wrong. The conversation shows the extent to which some Irish people let their hatred for England lead them to totally false perceptions of the world. Not all Irish people – not even the majority of them – thought as Pádraic did, but those who expressed such opinions damaged the image of good relations between Ireland and Germany.

In 1955, the correspondent Peter Grubbe wrote for *Die Welt* about the kindness of the Irish people towards the Germans. He reported that Germans in Ireland were always told the same stories:

> about German internees who fled from English POW camps in Northern Ireland and found refuge here, about German children who were fetched to Ireland after the war by Irish humanitarian work. And again and again the sentence is heard: about the old friendship between the Germans and the Irish.[69]

Grubbe commented on how well-liked Germans were in Ireland. He explained that the partition of the country had 'created parallels, had caused understanding [of the effects of the division of Germany] through an unnatural boundary'. Grubbe pointed out that Ireland and Germany had important trade links at their disposal which had become especially important after the loss of the German East. However, the article also contained many imprecisions on Irish politics and history, as did many other articles written by German correspondents based in Britain. For example, Grubbe wrote:

because of an unofficial alliance between the two countries [Germany
and Ireland], Ireland remained neutral in the war in spite of Allied
pressure and thus hindered the English fight against German sub-
marines.

The Irish policy of neutrality had certainly been the cause of bitter
complaints from the Allies, but to state that de Valera had kept Ireland
out of the war in order to benefit Germany is a pure myth, although
admittedly one that was popular in England immediately after the war.

One article about Ireland which appeared in the *Kölner Rundschau*
annoyed the German envoy to Ireland, Dr Katzenberger, so much that
he wrote an article himself to put right the errors it contained. The
article portrayed the Irish as a backward people who had never seen
a cinema and who only ate mutton. Hempel was presented as a
'Nazi-ambassador . . . who had reigned strictly over a considerable
German colony'.[70] Katzenberger wrote in reply:

> Apart from these facts, the article displays such errors and biased
> judgements, that I consider correction appropriate, given the friendly
> relations between Ireland and Germany . . . I observed none of these
> things [mentioned by the correspondent]. I did observe however the
> large and generous help which the Irish people gave to the German
> people in the truest Christian spirit after the war and is still giving
> now.[71]

One of the German journalists who took a great interest in Ireland in
the 1950s was Enno Stephan. He stayed in Ireland from 1953 to
1954 as a freelance journalist and wrote many articles about the
country in this time. Some of these were published by *Der Fortschritt*
as a series about Ireland. The series opened in June 1953 with the
following quotation:

> 'The Irish could teach the Germans to be disobedient, and if the
> Germans learnt to be disobedient, Europe could be saved.' Weighty
> sentences! which show the more than thousand year old relations
> between the two peoples, once begun by the monk Bonifatius, in a
> dramatic light. This thesis could explain why a small island on the edge
> of Europe, around the size of Bavaria and with only four and a half
> million people, was chosen as the subject of so much attention.[72]

Enno Stephan presented many different aspects of Irish life in his
articles. In the first, he dealt with the best-known of Irish problems,
partition.[73] He explained that Ireland had been living in a cold war

for thirty years. He described gerrymandering as an undemocratic process which disadvantaged Catholics in Northern Ireland. He recognised the similarities between Ireland and Germany and at the same time acknowledged the limitations of the analogy:

> What it Ulster? Is it like the Saar or eastern Upper Silesia for us? It is a poor comparison. The situation is more complicated than that, even if it does have astounding similarities with German problems.

Or: if the Irish could win against the English (he is referring to the War of Independence), was that not 'an example to Soviet-occupied central Germany'? He answered his question himself: 'London is not Moscow. An important factor for Ireland was public opinion in Great Britain and in the world.'[74] Through these examples Stephan showed that comparisons between the situations in Germany and Ireland could only go so far. He then asked the question as to who could help Ireland to achieve its aim, and answered that only America had the power to do this. Stephan concluded that Ireland was only damaging itself in the long term with its policy of neutrality:

> Will the Emerald Isle – and German fate also comes into question here – be able to demand and take in a world in which everything, including unity and freedom, has its price, without giving?[75]

On religion in Ireland Stephan wrote that Ireland, whose monks had contributed to christianising Germany, still remained the 'strongest treasure of the Christian West'.[76] Culturally, he wrote, the Gaelic League had been one of the driving forces in the fight for independence, and he mentioned the similarity to the influence of the Grimm brothers in forming a national identity in Germany: 'because we know the significance of the Grimm brothers in the growth of our nation, further explanation and discussion are superfluous.'[77] Stephan's articles reflected the general truth that German interest in Ireland was mainly in the areas of history and culture and not so much in politics, as many Irish officials hoped it would be.

The IRA attacks which took place in this period did receive considerable coverage by the German press. The newspaper *Christ und Welt* published an article about the movement in 1954.[78] In it the reporter concluded that the age of Irish nationalism was over and that the Irish government had long since recognised this fact. He did show some understanding for the aims of the IRA:

> The IRA, in an era of world-wide ideological debate . . . has become a
> further curiosity in Europe, one of many in this area rich in curiosities.
> One cannot help but sympathise, not with their methods, but with
> their traditions which were forged during the colonial period in a
> suppressed people's fight for freedom.

In the *Stuttgarter Zeitung* the IRA was condemned for trying 'to
reach a solution of the Irish question by force in the age of self-
determination'.[79] This view reflects that expressed in many German
newspapers. Ireland's voluntary isolation from NATO and the IRA
attempts to solve the problem of partition through violence met with
a lack of sympathy in the international climate of the 1950s.

Although most articles in German newspapers portrayed Ireland in
a positive light, there were some which contained unfriendly or even
false reports. In 1955, after reports on an IRA attack near London
containing false information about Ireland appeared in many newspapers, Kiernan, the Irish envoy in Bonn, recommended that the Irish
government publish a leaflet about partition in German. He stated
that he would personally see that the leaflet reached the right people
in Germany.[80] Kiernan also reported that Dr Hempel, the former
German envoy to Dublin, was involved in assuring that incorrect
information about Ireland was refuted:

> Dr Hempel . . . has called on me and in the course of conversation he
> referred to the ignorance of the German people, including the press,
> concerning Ireland, about which the vaguest and often most absurd
> views were held. He said that he had himself corrected his friends in
> the newspaper world on many occasions.[81]

An article published in the newspaper *Vorwärts* is an example of this
kind of uninformed journalism:

> . . . Éire's neutrality caused great damage through the refusal of the use
> . . . of Irish harbours for convoy purposes (which cost the lives of ten
> thousands of British seamen) and the suffering of widely ramified Nazi
> spying organisations on Irish soil . . . Fine Gael [wishes] the return of
> Ireland into the British Commonwealth . . . Sinn Féin is . . . a completely
> fascist movement, down to details of organisation . . . The fascists
> want all or nothing.[82]

The Irish legation sent a letter of protest to the newspaper:

> If you must get your news on a country which maintains friendly relations with the Federal Republic from England, then the least that can be expected is that you ensure that the articles do not contain distorted portrayals.[83]

The fact that the article was written by Benjamin Carr, the London correspondent of the newspaper, confirms that the Irish government was justified in being concerned about German newspapers reporting on Ireland from British sources.

In an article in the *Deutsche Volkszeitung*[84] the following was reported:

> The Catholic church keeps the Irish population in ignorance or semi-educated. This explains the Irish affinity for Hitler's fascism. Siemens built Irish electrical plants at an early stage. Not only German specialists were working on the construction. According to a whispering campaign, Hitler's victory over England was unavoidable.

The electricity plant was built by Siemens in 1929. How there could have been a whispering campaign about Hitler's victory then was not explained. This report had also been written by a London correspondent. Such articles annoyed the Irish authorities considerably and led to more information about Ireland being distributed in Germany by Irish government sources in an attempt to combat such reporting.

German journalists were very interested in Ireland's views on the Atlantic alliance. The Irish position on this issue had been made clear by the Irish Minister for External Affairs, MacBride, when Ireland was invited in 1949 to become a member of NATO. It was impossible for Ireland to become a member, he said, as long as 'six of her counties are occupied by British forces against the will of the overwhelming majority of the Irish people'.[85] Ireland hoped to move the issue of partition into a central position and to gain American support for the unification of the country through this policy. Even those Irish politicians who carried out this policy must have known that it had no chance of success. Ireland reaped more scorn than sympathy for this move. The events after the war had already damaged relations with America, so the chances were even smaller that America would support Ireland's strategy.

In 1951–52 many articles were published in Germany about Ireland's policy of neutrality. The Catholic newspaper *Rheinische Merkur*, accused Ireland of living in 'splendid isolation' and claimed that Ireland had turned its back on Europe.[86] In 1949 *Die Zeit* wrote about Ireland's decision to become a Republic in relation to the consequences of this for the Atlantic military pact.[87] According to the journalist, the island represented an irreparable gap to the west of England's defences.

In 1955 the *Münchner Merkur* sent a reporter to Ireland to interview the then Taoiseach, John A. Costello. The reporter was above all interested in Ireland's stance on important foreign issues. In order to answer his questions on this matter, Costello emphasised the position which was frequently cited in these years when Ireland's foreign policy was addressed: that Ireland despised Communism but that the country could not join NATO as long as it was partitioned. To overcome partition was the dominant problem of the country, just as was reunification for Germany.[88]

These excerpts from various German newspapers provide a view of the image of Ireland which was produced by the German media. This image was, as has been seen, very varied. The main view was, however, the picture of the inhabitants of the 'Emerald Isle' as romantic, friendly people who took a great interest in their own history and also in that of Germany. These articles led to a greater knowledge about Ireland, and especially to considerable interest in Ireland as a travel destination. On a cultural level, the newspaper articles played a role in the revival and increase in German interest in Ireland as the country of Celtic history, literature and music. But many of them created an idealised image which Germans wished to project onto Ireland – a place that was green, natural, romantic, unhurried and slightly wild – everything that they felt Germany at the time was not.

CHAPTER SEVEN

Summary

German–Irish relations must be seen from various different points of view, as has been illustrated here. The personal relations between the two peoples, the contacts between the Irish government and the Allies regarding German questions, and the relations between the Federal Republic and the Republic of Ireland have to be judged separately. One of the main questions which arose in this book – namely whether the relations were dominated by politics in the period examined – can be answered in the affirmative. Research has clearly shown that politics represented a permanent issue in German–Irish humanitarian, economic or cultural relations.

It must be stressed that the particular emphasis on politics in the contacts between Ireland and Germany was mostly initiated by the Irish side. It can be said that the difficult, sometimes bitter, relations between Ireland and Britain often influenced German–Irish relations. During and immediately after the Second World War, Ireland's relations with America were also clouded, since the Irish government felt that the independence of the country was being ignored by the USA and by Britain, for example when the Allies demanded to be allowed to use the Irish ports, or when they insisted on the deportation of the German spies to Germany. The desire to prove that Ireland could act independently of any outside pressure, that the country was independent de facto as well as de jure, influenced relations with Germany on humanitarian, diplomatic, economic and cultural levels.

The way in which the Irish government dealt with German citizens in Ireland during and after the war caused furore and condemnations from abroad. In particular, the question of German soldiers, spies and diplomats became an issue of contention between Ireland and the Allies. De Valera's aim was to afford these people protection, and it was an aim that was approved of by the Irish people who knew what it was like to be on the losing side. De Valera's main motive, however, was to use the issue to demonstrate Irish independence. This way of thinking in terms of national interest above all else remained predominant well into the 1960s and resulted in Ireland's isolation in the international sphere in the 1950s.

The accusation frequently raised in Britain that Irish humanitarian aid for Germany was given for political reasons was untrue. There is no doubt that some people saw the situation in Germany as a chance to help an enemy of Britain's and so were blind to the crimes of the Third Reich. To conclude from this that the majority of the Irish people donated food, clothes and money or fostered German children for political reasons would be to place Irish humanitarian aid for Germany in a dubious light and would be completely unjust. The aid for Germany in the 1940s was a gesture of sympathy which led to the development of strong ties between the two countries in the following years.

While the accusation that the Irish population had a predominantly political interest in Germany can be considered false, it did apply to a large number of Irish politicians, particularly to members of Fianna Fáil. Irish partition was the main topic of Irish politics, at least rhetorically: 'Wherever he spoke, de Valera's repeated message was on the need to end partition'.[1] Germany was one of the most important target countries for Irish propaganda against partition. Issues which only concerned economics or culture were turned into political topics by Irish politicians. The strategy could not claim any considerable success politically: in the Europe of the 1950s it was, in fact, considered nationalistic and backward by many. The predominance of politics at a government level did not, however, mean that the economic, diplomatic and cultural relations between Ireland and Germany were of no importance or were not sufficiently developed.

The financial support for, and the interest which Irish politicians showed in, German authors and academics contributed to a greater knowledge in Ireland about Germany, and vice-versa. The Irish–German and German–Irish societies, the German school in Dublin and the lively academic exchanges between Ireland and Germany, all played a role in the development of deeper relations between the two peoples and also, in a small way, led to the gradual opening up of Irish society to Europe.

Irish trade with Germany can also be viewed in the light of the political aims that dominated the relations in general. It is clear that one of the main aims of trade with Germany was to reduce economic dependence on Britain – this target was not reached in the period in question here. Markets on the Continent did play an increasingly important role for Ireland in the 1950s, but Britain remained firmly at the top of the list. The fact that the quantitative trade with Germany was not of great importance does not mean that the relations were not of importance qualitatively. Post-war trade relations differed from those before the war in that they were developed on a much more personal level. Irish businesspeople took part in trade fairs in Germany, German companies were set up in Ireland; and Düsseldorf developed into a small but lively Irish trade centre in Germany – this kind of contact had not existed before the war. In the following years trade with Germany took on an increasingly important role.

Summing up, it can be said that the importance of politics that was emphasised by the Irish government did not have anywhere near the importance in German–Irish relations which some politicians strove for. It was the cultural and economic relations and the personal contacts between German and Irish people which deepened and strengthened in the period examined here.

Notes

CHAPTER ONE

1 Memorandum from the Irish Minister for Industry and Commerce, no date, DFA 314/10/6.
2 Duggan, John P., *Neutral Ireland and the Third Reich*, p. xiv.
3 These men were part of the British army.
4 Coogan, Tim Pat, *De Valera*, p. 62.
5 Ibid., p. 110.
6 These details were supplied by Enno Stephan, both in his book and in interviews with the author.

CHAPTER TWO

1 Carter, Carolle, J., 'The spy who brought his lunch', in: *Eire-Ireland*, Vol. 10, p. 3.
2 Keogh, Dermot, *Twentieth Century Ireland*, p. 110.
3 Smyllie, R. M., 'Unneutral Neutral Eire', in: *Foreign Affairs* No. 24, 1945–1946, p. 320.
4 Enno Stephan to the author.
5 Heinrich Becker shares this opinion.
6 From: G2, Dept of Defence, 19 October 1940 to Chief Superintendent, Garda HQ, Kilmainham, G2/X/2053.
7 From: Garda Detective Branch, 8 October 1940, G2/X/2053.
8 Quoted in a Garda Detective Branch report, 8 October 1940, G2/X/2053.
9 From: Garda Detective Branch, 2 December 1940, G2/X/2053.
10 Stephan, Enno, *Spies in Ireland*, p. 269.
11 From a report written by W. D. Klübers. Made available by Eberhard Langer.
12 From Klüber's report.
13 Irish Red Cross files, 25.2.1944.
14 Taken from a list of prisoners, April 1945, DFA 241/309.
15 From Klüber's report.
16 From Klüber's report.
17 Letter from Sir John Maffey to the Secretary of External Affairs, 14 June 1945, DFA A71.
18 Irish government report, 29 October 1946, DFA A34.
19 *Irish Times*, 6 August 1945.
20 Dwyer, T. Ryle, *Guests of the State*, p. 236.
21 Duggan, John P., *Neutral Ireland and the Third Reich*, p. 247.

22 From Klüber's report.
23 Carroll, Joseph T., *Ireland in the War Years*, p. 61.
24 Stephan, p. 124.
25 *Der Spiegel*, 6 December 1961, No. 50, p. 64.
26 Report by Conor Cruise O'Brien, 29 September 1954, DFA A34.
27 Görtz' statement, quoted in Stephan, p. 87.
28 Stephan, p. 83.
29 Stephan, p. 105.
30 Quoted in Stephan, p. 117.
31 From a Comparison of Görtz statement of 2.10.45 with Garda document of Dec. 1944, p. 2, Military Archives, Dublin
32 Stephan, p. 227.
33 Report from 28 November 1941, DFA A34.
34 Archives Dept, University College Dublin, P21/142.
35 Memorandum from the British Secretary of State, 5 April 1945, PRO DO 35 WX 130/3/40.
36 *Irish Independent*, 9 April 1945.
37 Telegram from Maffey to the British government, 3 May 1945, PRO WX 130/3/40.
38 Quoted in Coogan, Tim Pat, *De Valera*, p. 610.
39 Letter from J. M. Troutbeck, British Foreign Office, to M. E. Allen, Dominions Office, 17 May 1945, PRO DO 35 WX 130/3/40.
40 Letter from M. E. Allen, 6 December 1945, PRO DO WX 130/3/40.
41 Memorandum from Joseph Walshe, 14 June 1945, DFA A74.
42 Letter from Hempel to Boland, 14 May 1946, DFA A54.
43 Brief von John Leydon, Wirtschaftministerium, an Joseph Walshe, 15 Oktober 1945, DFA A 62.
44 Memorandum der irischen Polizei, 13 Sept. 1946, DFA A62.
45 Memorandum from David Gray to his government, 24 June 1946, DFA A54.
46 Letter from the American Embassy in Britain to the British Foreign Office, 25 Ocober 1946, PRO FO 371/55358.
47 Letter from the British Foreign Office to the Dominions Office, 7 November 1946, PRO FO 371/55358.
48 Memorandum from the Foreign Office, 24 June 1946, PRO FO 371/55351.
49 Letters from those affected to the British government, PRO FO 371/55358.
50 Memorandum from the British Representative in Ireland, 18 April 1946, PRO FO 371/55350.
51 *Twentieth Century Ireland*, p. 111.
52 Report from Dan Bryan to the Minister for Defence, DFA A71.
53 Dan Bryan, ibid.
54 Ibid.
55 Letter to Bryan, 23 May 1946, DFA A7.
56 Letter from Sir John Maffey to the Secretary of External Affairs, 14 June 1945, DFA A71.

57 Letter from J. P. Walshe to Sir John Maffey, 22 June 1945, DFA A71.
58 Ibid.
59 Note on a telegram from Maffey to the Secretary of State for Dominion Affairs, 22 June 1945, DFA A7.
60 Letter from the British Foreign Office to the Economic Warfare Department, 12 November 1946, FO 371/55354.
61 Letter from Görtz to the Irish Department of Justice, 25 June 1945, DFA A71.
62 Protocol from 20 October 1945 from Roche, Department of Justice, to External Affairs, DFA A71.
63 Letter from Boland to the Secretary of the Department of Justice, 21 September 1945, DFA A7.
64 Letter to David Gray, not dated, DFA A7.
65 Stephan, p. 272
66 Letter from the French government to the President of Ireland, 25 March 1946, PRO FO 341/55349.
67 This opinion was presented in a protocol of the Dominions Office from 20 August 1946, FO 371/55353.
68 Ibid.
69 Duggan, John P., *Neutral Ireland and the Third Reich*, p. 245.
70 Letter from the American Embassy to the British Foreign Office, 25 October 1946, FO 371/55358.
71 Letter to de Valera, 29 October 1946. Probably written by the Secretary of External Affairs. DFA A7.
72 Fisk, Robert, *In Time of War*.
73 Report from External Affairs to foreign representatives in Ireland, 22 April 1947, DFA A71.
74 External Affairs report, no date, DFA A34.
75 Stephan, p. 275.
76 Information supplied by Enno Stephan, March 1997.
77 Memorandum from External Affairs, 18 May 1949, DFA 318/6.
78 *Der Spiegel*, 1950, p. 20.
79 Enno Stephan to the author.
80 Letter from Bruchans to External Affairs, 6 February 1950, DFA A74.
81 Duggan, *Neutral Ireland and the Third Reich*, p. 250.
82 Letter from the Irish Department of Justice to External Affairs, 11 February 1947, DFA 410/45.
83 *Guests of the State*, p. 243.
84 Letter from Arthur Jackel, 25 April 1947, DFA 410/45/8.
85 Letter from Habicht to an Irish friend, 11 October 1946, DFA 410/45/8.
86 From W. D. Klüber's speech to the guests at the Maritime Museum in Dun Laoghaire, 27 May 1994. Made available by Eberhardt Langer.
87 *Cork Examiner*, 30 April 1995.
88 Letter from Hans Karsch to Eberhard Langer, December 1995. Made available by Eberhard Langer.
89 Speech by Hellmut Karsch in the Curragh Camp Headquarters, 28 May 1994. Made available by Eberhard Langer.

90 Letter from Katzenberger to the Foreign Office in Bonn, 4 December 1951, AA 516–01–33 II.
91 Letter from Katzenberger to the Foreign Office, 12 July 1952, AA 516–01–33 II.
92 Letter sent by the Kriegsgräberverein, found in the Goethe Institute, Dublin.
93 Interview with Mrs and Mr Clissmann, November 1994.

CHAPTER THREE

1 Bark, Dennis L., and Gress, David R., *A History of West Germany*, p. 23
2 Harald Zink, quoted in Bark and Gress, p. 26
3 Flamm, Dr. Franz, (ed.), *Die Auslandshilfe für die Stadt Freiburg im Breisgau 1945–1949*, p. 11.
4 Wollasch, Hans-Josef, *Humanitäre Auslandshilfe für Deutschland nach dem Zweiten Weltkrieg*, p. 38.
5 *Irish Times*, 29 May 1945.
6 *Irish Press*, 2 August 1945.
7 *Irish Press*, 5 October 1945.
8 *Die Zeit* No. 24, 7 June 1996.
9 Letter from Dr Nuelle, Caritas to C. Cremin, External Affairs, 12 February 1948, DFA 419/1/7B.
10 Caritas memorandum, 4 September 1947, Caritas Archive 371(–87) Fasz. 3K.
11 Wirtschaftszeitung, Stuttgart, 18 April 1947, Caritas Archive 371 (–87) Fasz.3K.
12 Letter from Cardinal Faulhaber to the President of Ireland, 17 March 1948, Caritas Archive 371(–87) Fasz.3K. Author's translation.
13 Friedrichs, Werner, *Ein deutsches Denkmal im Stephen's Green*, p. 5. Author's translation.
14 *Limerick Chronicle*, 21 March 1946.
15 *Irish Press*, 4 October 1945.
16 Friedrichs, p. 5.
17 *Irish Times*, 6 October 1945.
18 Letter from External Affairs, 15 January 1947, DFA 410/1/257.
19 *Irish Times*, 3 October 1945.
20 *Irish Times*, March 1946.
21 *Irish Press*, 11 October 1947.
22 Text in the Irish–Jewish Museum, Dublin.
23 Keogh, Dermot, *Twentieth Century Ireland*, p. 166.
24 From Werner Stephan's diary. By kind permission of Enno Stephan.
25 Sachsen, Ernst Heinrich Prinz von, *Mein Lebensweg vom Königsschloß zum Bauernhof*, p. 307.
26 Quoted in the *Irish Times*, 21 January 1946.

27 Letter from G2 staff, Southern Command, Cork, 12 February 1946. G2/X/1500.

28 *Cork Examiner*, 31 January 1951.

29 *Cork Examiner*, 16 June 1951.

30 *Cork Examiner*, 3 December 1951.

31 *Irish Times*, 17 October 1945.

32 Ibid.

33 Ibid.

34 Friedrichs, p. 6.

35 Quoted in *Irish Times*, 20 October 1945.

36 Report from 18 October 1945, DFA 419/6.

37 Including for example 'Maisie Donnelly, her sister and her mother . . . associates of escaped German internees . . . Miss Nancy Whelan, associated with escaped German internees . . . Kevin C. Cahill, associated with the Irish Friends of Germany and Coras na bPoblachta organisations, Thomas Hunt . . . ex-IRA prisoner, Miss Annie O'Farrell, was engaged to Sean Russell.' Ibid.

38 Report from External Affairs, 18 October 1945, DFA 419/6.

39 Dáil Debates, Vol. 91, columns 569–72, 9 July 1943, quoted in Keogh, p. 130.

40 Memorandum for the Minister for External Affairs, 13 February 1946, DFA 419/6.

41 External Affairs file, 18 October 1945, DFA 419/6.

42 Police report, 18 October 1945, DFA 419/6.

43 Keogh, p. 129.

44 Quoted in the *Irish Times*, 20 October 1945.

45 *Irish Times*, 20 October 1945.

46 Letter from Isolde Farrell to the Minister for External Affairs, 10 December 1945.

47 E.g. *Irish Independent*, 14 December 1945 'Starving Children', *Irish Independent*, 19 December 1945; 'Bray's interest in German Children', *Irish Independent*, 25 January 1946.

48 *Irish Independent*, 19 December 1945.

49 *Irish Independent*, 21 December 1945.

50 *Irish Independent*, 19 December 1945.

51 *Irish Press*, 8 January 1946.

52 Quoted in the *Irish Independent*, 25 January 1946.

53 E.g. in a letter from Martin McNamara to Isolde Farrell, 11 February 1946, DFA 419/6.

54 Memorandum for External Affairs, 13 February 1946, DFA 419/6.

55 Ibid. In 1947 Hermann Görtz, who had been interned in Ireland for spying, became secretary of the Save the German Children Society for a short time. Since the Allies wanted his deportation, his employment meant further damage to the Society's image.

56 Interview with Enno Stephan, April 1995.

57 *Irish Times*, 20 February 1946.

58 British report on the meeting, PRO FO 371/55521.

59 Letter from Isolde Farrell to J. P. Walshe, 8 March 1946, DFA 419/6.
60 Letter from 16 March 1946, DFA 419/6.
61 Letter from Brown to Troutbeck, 29 April 1946, PRO FO 371/55521.
62 Letter from Troutbeck to Brown, 30 April 1946, PRO FO 371/55521.
63 Letter from External Affairs to the Secretary of the Red Cross, 31 May 1946, DFA 419/6.
64 Ibid.
65 Letter from the Dominions Office to Maffey, 26 June 1946, PRO FO 371/55521.
66 *Limerick Chronicle*, 30 April 1946.
67 *Irish Press*, 3 June 1946.
68 External Affairs report, 3 June 1946, DFA 419/6.
69 Memorandum for External Affairs, 4 June 1946, DFA 419/6.
70 Memorandum for External Affairs, 6 June 1946, DFA 419/6.
71 Letter from Isolde Farrell to the Secretary of External Affairs, 4 June 1946, DFA 419/6.
72 Irish Red Cross report, 14 June 1946, Red Cross Archive.
73 List of available families, Save the German Children Society, DFA 419/6.
74 Conference notes of 29 June 1946, 2 July 1946, DFA 419/6.
75 Letter from External Affairs to Department of Justice, 3 July 1946, DFA 419/6.
76 Unsigned memorandum for External Affairs, 15 July 1946, DFA 419/6.
77 Ibid.
78 Irish Red Cross report, no date, Red Cross archives.
79 Unsigned memorandum, 30 July 1946, DFA 419/6.
80 Unsigned letter, 31 August 1946, DFA 419/6.
81 Letter from Martin McNamara to Conor Cremin, 5 September 1946, DFA 419/6.
82 Maurice Stormer to Rod MacHugh, 9 March 1949, DFA 419/6.
83 Red Cross file, Central Council Minutes No. 3, 25 October 1946.
84 Ernest Berkenheiers to the author, August 1996.
85 Red Cross file, Central Council Minutes No. 3, 15 November 1946.
86 Red Cross file, Executive Committee Minutes No. 3, 2 April 1947.
87 Letter from Dr K. Joerger, Director of Caritas, to Baron Livonius, 22 May 1947, German Caritas Archive R76/1.
88 Translation of a report by an unnamed Red Cross worker, published in the Wirtschaftszeitung, Stuttgart, 18 April 1947.
89 Interview with Ursula Weber in Glencree, 24 March 1997.
90 Letter from Dr Firmenich, Diocesan Caritas Director, Aachen, to Caritas in Freiburg, 20 April 1949, German Caritasverband Archive 371 (–87) Fasz. 3K.
91 Interview with Declan Finnucan, nephew of Paddy, in Glencree, 24 March 1997.
92 Red Cross file, Chairman's Reports Meetings, 26 November 1948.
93 Red Cross file, Chairman's Reports Meetings, 29 April 1949.
94 Interview with Mr and Mrs Clissmann, November 1994.

95 'Kinder ohne Muttersprache' by Enno Stephan, in *Der Fortschritt* No. 26, 26 June 1953.

96 According to information supplied by Mr McQuillan, Swords, July 1996.

97 According to the wishes of the person concerned no name has been included here.

98 Red Cross file, Chairman's Reports Meetings, 26 November 1948.

99 Caritas Archive, 20 April 1949, 371(–87) Fasz. 3K.

100 Red Cross file, Chairman's Reports Meetings, 26 November 1948.

101 Interview with Enno Stephan, April 1995.

102 Interview with Mr and Mrs Clissmann, November 1994.

103 *Irish Independent*, 29 July 1996.

104 Letter from the Save the German Children Society to External Affairs, 28 February 1949, DFA 419/6.

105 Letter from Oliver J. Flanagan, TD to Seán MacBride, 5 March 1949, DFA 419/6.

106 Unsigned memorandum from External Affairs, 30 May 1949, DFA 419/6.

107 External Affairs report, 30 May 1949, DFA 419/6.

108 Friedrichs, p. 9.

109 Reader's letter to the *Evening Mail*, 22 June 1951.

110 E.g. the story in the *Enniscorthy Echo* on 3 February 1952 about a child who returned in 1952, or Ernest Berkenheier who couldn't get used to Germany and became an Irish citizen (Berkenheier to the author).

111 Letter from Moritz O'Connor, 25 September 1950, AA 304.

112 *The Bulletin*, Vol. 3, July–August 1950, p. 5, AA 304.

113 Ibid.

114 Report by Herr Kordt to the Save the German Children Society, 27 November 1950, AA 411–02/33.

115 Appendix to Report No. 411 of the German Legation in Dublin to the Foreign Office in Bonn, 11 January 1952, AA 310–12/II.

116 Ibid.

117 Report from the German Legation to Bonn, 22 January 1952, AA 310–12 II.

118 Herbert Remmel to the author, August 1996.

119 From a speech by Theodor Heuss, 27 November 1951, quoted in *Dankspende des deutschen Volkes*, Berlin 1955, p. 15.

120 Report on the last meeting of the Dankspende des deutschen Volkes on 11 January 1957. Supplied by Enno Stephan.

121 *Irish Independent*, 11 December 1953.

122 Seán O'Ceallaigh in a letter to Theodor Heuss, 9 February 1950, DFA 338/413.

123 Theodor Heuss in a letter to Seán O'Ceallaigh, DFA 338/413.

124 Protocol of Katzenberger's speech, 28 January 1956, DFA 338/314.

125 Werner Stephan's diary, 28 January 1956.With the kind permission of Enno Stephan.
126 Letter from the German Legation to Bonn, 19 January 1956, DFA 338/314.
127 *Dankspende des deutschen Volkes*, p. 228.

CHAPTER FOUR

1 *Irish Trade Journal*, June 1947, p. 81.
2 Report by the two representatives, March 1949, DFA 314/10/6.
3 Memorandum from External Affairs, 2 May 1950, DFA 317/47.
4 Telegram from Belton, 28 October 1950, DFA 319/29.
5 Report from Belton to External Affairs, 1 December 1950, DFA 318/6/1.
6 Memorandum from Kordt, 18 January 1951, Foreign Office, Bonn 210–02/33.
7 Speech by Belton in Bonn, 11 June 1951, DFA 317/47/1.
8 Speech by Katzenberger in Dublin, 26 July 1951, DFA 317/47/1.
9 Report by Katzenberger to Bonn, 31 July 1951, AA 210–02/33.
10 *The Standard*, 3 August 1951.
11 Memorandum from the Irish government, 22 March 1951, DFA 314/10/6.
12 Report by William Fay (from the Irish trade delegation), 9 September 1951, DFA 314/49.
13 Ireland, *Bulletin of the Department of External Affairs*, No. 77, March 1951, published in Dublin.
14 Central Statistics Office, Trade and Shipping Statistics 1938–1957, Dublin.
15 *The Bulletin*, No. 152, 8 September 1952.
16 Report by Katzenberger to Bonn, 5 September 1952, AA 752–05/33 9410.
17 Ibid.
18 Ibid.
19 *Merkblätter für den deutschen Außenhandel: Irland, hrsg. im Auftrage der Bundesauskunftsstelle für den Außenhandel*, Köln 1953, p. 9.
20 *The Bulletin*, No. 77, March 1951.
21 Irish Trade Statistics 1948–1957, Dublin.
22 *Daily Herald*, 2 August 1955.
23 Keogh, Dermot, *Twentieth Century Ireland*, p. 215.
24 Weekly Index of Would Events, Keynshaw (Bristol), Keesing Publications 1931, *Keesing's Contemporary Archives*, 16–23 June 1956, p. 14, 927.

CHAPTER FIVE

1 Sagarra, Eda, *Dreißig Jahre Bundesrepublik*, p. 101.
2 Becker, Heinrich, *In Memorium*, Maurice O'Connor, Düren 1970, unpublished manuscript.
3 Elisabeth Clissmann to the author, November 1994.
4 Bryan, 3 October 1947, DFA P11.
5 Kriegsmärchen in Irland (1939–1945), in *H. Becker, Neue Blüten des ungezogenen Kaktus*, unpublished manuscript.
6 Quoted in an Irish government memorandum, 26 November 1944, DFA 238/337.
7 From the opening speech of the Irish–German Society, 29 October 1951, AA 400–21–33 VI.
8 Report by Katzenberger to Bonn, 30 November 1954, AA 400–21.
9 Bulletin of the Irish–German Society, December 1951. Own translation
10 Memorandum from the Cultural Department in Bonn, 12 January 1952, AA 400–21–33 VI.
11 *The Bulletin*, November 1953, p. 3.
12 Memorandum by the Cultural Department in Bonn, 13 March 1952, AA 400–21–33 VI.
13 Ibid., 1 August 1953, AA 400–21–33 VI.
14 Ibid.
15 *Irish Independent*, 28 October 1952.
16 Letter from the Cultural Department in Bonn to Katzenberger, AA 400–21–33 VI.
17 Report by Katzenberger, 26 February 1953, AA 400–21–33 VI. Own translation.
18 Stephan to the author, April 1995. Author's translation
19 M. Flesch, in *Bulletin of the German–Irish Society*, published in Dublin, September 1953. Author's translation. AA 400–21–33 VI
20 Dr Adolph Reifferscheidt from the German Embassy in Ireland, in the 'Frankfurter Allgemeine Zeitung', 1 May 1961.
21 Belton to External Affairs, 2 April 1952, DFA 414/94.
22 Memorandum of the Irish–German Society, 31 December 1953, DFA P8/1.
23 Bryan, 3 October 1947, DFA P11.
24 Nunan to Belton, July 1953, DFA P11.
25 Memorandum of the German–Irish Society, 19 June 1954, DFA P8/1.
26 Letter from the Dublin Grand Opera Society to External Affairs, 20 February 1950, DFA 338/210.
27 Letter from Katzenberger to the Foreign Office in Bonn, 29 June 1954, AA 450–04.
28 E.g. in the *Rundschau Bonn*, 3 November 1954.
29 *Diplomatischer Kurier*, 1955, p. 328.
30 Letter from the Irish Minister for Education, 26 September 1951, DFA 324/20/19.

31 Letter from the Irish Legation to External Affairs, 22 July 1954, DFA 324/20/19.
32 Letter from the *BayerischerJugendring* to External Affairs, 22 November 1955, DFA 324/20/19.
33 *Bulletin*, No. 85, 21 May 1951.
34 6 July 1951, AA 471–03/9410.

CHAPTER SIX

1 Articles 2 and 3 of the Irish Constitution, quoted in Coogan, Tim Pat, *De Valera*, p. 492. Author's italics.
2 *The Bulletin*, No. 185, 4 May 1953.
3 Report from Katzenberger to the Foreign Ministry, 3 December 1951, AA 211–00/33.
4 Letter from Conor Cruise O'Brien to Patrick Lynch, 23 November 1949, DFA 438/62.
5 Keogh, Dermot, *Twentieth Century Ireland*, p. 201.
6 Letter from Belton to External Affairs, 11 February 1952, DFA 316/202.
7 Letter from Belton, 17 January 1952.
8 Wittig to Belton, 20 December 1951, DFA 323/34/2.
9 Belton to Fógra Failte, 17 February 1954, DFA 323/34/2.
10 Letter from the Irish Legation in Bonn to External Affairs, 11 October 1954, DFA 323/34/2.
11 Letter from Gerstenberger to Conor Cruise O'Brien, 31 October 1949, DFA 438/62.
12 Ibid.
13 Coogan, p. 641.
14 'Was ist Partition?', no date, DFA 438/62.
15 Letter from Conor Cruise O'Brien, 23 November 1949, DFA 438/62.
16 Letter from Professor Heiermeier to the Cultural Relations Committee, 6 November 1949, DFA 438/61.
17 Ibid.
18 Letter from John Belton, 21 March 1951, DFA 438/167.
19 Letter from John Belton, 22 May 1952, 438/21/23.
20 As this book was being prepared, it was revealed that Klaus Volkmann had been a member of the NSDAP and had been responsible for the death of Jews in Poland during the war. In 1948 he adopted the pseudonym Peter Grubbe and became London correspondent of the *Frankfurter Allgemeine Zeitung*. This information is from *Die Zeit* No. 42, 13 October 1995.
21 Letter from Conor Cruise O'Brien to Frank Gallagher, Government Information Bureau, 5 April 1954, DFA 406/79.
22 Letter from Klaus Volkmann to Conor Cruise O'Brien, 31 March 1954, DFA 406/79.
23 Gallagher, Frank, *The Indivisible Island*, Gollancz, London 1957.
24 Dickl, Horst, *Die deutsche Außenpolitik*, May 1958, p. 495.

25 Dpa report on the book *The Indivisible Island*, 27 January 1958, DFA P/2/8/A.

26 Letter from Kiernan to External Affairs, 13 December 1957, DFA P/2/8/A.

27 Letter from Kiernan to External Affairs, 29 August 1955, DFA D21.

28 Letter from Conor Cruise O'Brien to Aedan O'Beirne, 13 August 1952, DFA 414/82.

29 *Irlands Recht auf Einheit*, p. 1.

30 Letter from Belton to External Affairs, 24 April 1951, DFA 318/6/1.

31 Report from Katzenberger to the Foreign Office, 3 December 1951, AA 211–00/33.

32 Ibid., 14 January 1952, AA 602–04/33.

33 Letter from the Foreign Office to Katzenberger, 1 February 1952, DFA 602–04/33.

34 Ibid., 14 January 1952, AA 602–14/33 Abt.III.

35 Letter from Dr. Schirmer, Press and Information Department of the Federal Government, to the Foreign Office, 14 August 1952, AA 602–04/33.

36 Letter from John Belton to External Affairs, 25 July 1955, DFA D/2.

37 Letter from the German Legation, Dublin, to the Press and Information Dept., Bonn, 20 August 1954, AA 310.752–05.

38 Report from 28 September 1954, DFA 436/69.

39 Report from the Press and Information Dept. to the Foreign Office, 31 October 1951, AA, 602–04/33.

40 Report from Richthofen, July 1953, AA 205–00/33.

41 Bark, Dennis L. and Gress, David R., *A History of West Germany*, p. 155.

42 Letter from Brian Durnin to Conor Cruise O'Brien, 18 January 1952, DFA 432/16.

43 Coogan, p. 408.

44 Comment made by von Richthofen, 14 July 1955, AA 602–04/94.10.

45 Sagarra, Eda, *Dreißig Jahre Bundesrepublik*, p. 107.

46 Keogh, p. 198.

47 Ibid., p. 198.

48 Ibid., p. 200.

49 Report from Katzenberger to the Foreign Office, 18 December 1952, AA 211–00/33 II.

50 *Limerick Leader*, 20 July 1953.

51 *Irish Times*, 17 August 1955.

52 *Irish Times*, 1 July 1952.

53 Letter from Katzenberger to the Foreign Office, 1 July 1952, AA 602–04/33.

54 *Irish Times*, 23 October 1951.

55 *Irish Independent*, 31 August and 2 September 1955.

56 *Irish Independent*, 2 September 1955.

57 *Irish Independent*, 31 August 1955.

58 Letter from Belton to Gerald Boland, Minister for Justice, 13 September 1952, DFA A/6.
59 *Illus*, No. 44, Berlin, 5 November 1950.
60 Letter from Belton to External Affairs, 2 November 1950, DFA D21.
61 Kiernan's report to External Affairs, 21 December 1951, DFA D19.
62 Report by von Richthofen, July 1953, AA 205–00/33.
63 *Lichtenfelser Tageblatt*, 23 December 1954.
64 *Mannheimer Morgen*, 15 September 1955.
65 *Lichtenfelser Tageblatt*, 23 December 1954.
66 *Die Zeit*, 18 March 1948.
67 Böll, Heinrich, in *Nachwort zum Irischen Tagebuch*, p. 125.
68 Ibid., p. 39.
69 *Die Welt*, 8 August 1955.
70 *Kölner Rundschau*, 16 November 1952.
71 *Kölner Rundschau*, 30 November 1952.
72 *Der Fortschritt*, June 1953.
73 *Der Fortschritt*, No. 25, 19 June 1953, p. 4.
74 *Der Fortschritt*, No. 34, 21 August 1953.
75 *Der Fortschritt*, No. 25.
76 *Der Fortschritt*, No. 35.
77 *Der Fortschritt*, No. 35.
78 *Christ und Welt*, 8 September 1955.
79 *Stuttgarter Zeitung*, quoted in a report on the German Press by Brian O'Ceallaigh, German Legation, to External Affairs, 7 September 1955, DFA D/21.
80 Report by Kiernan to External Affairs, 23 August 1955, DFA D/21.
81 Ibid., 2 September 1955 DFA D/21.
82 Translation of an article from *Vorwärts*, 30 September 1955, DFA D21
83 Letter from Brian O'Ceallaigh to the chief editor, 10 October 1955, DFA D21.
84 *Deutsche Volkszeitung*, 2 March 1957.
85 Quoted in Keogh, p. 193.
86 *Rheinischer Merkur*, 18 April 1952.
87 *Die Zeit*, 20 January 1949.
88 *Münchner Merkur*, 16/17 July 1955.

CHAPTER SEVEN

1 Keogh, Dermot, *Twentieth Century Ireland*, p. 192.

Sources and bibliography

ARCHIVE MATERIAL

National Archives, Dublin
   DFA: Department of Foreign Affairs
Military Archives, Dublin
   G2 Documents
Public Record Office, Kew, London
   FO 371: Foreign Office
   DO 35: Dominions Office
Politisches Archiv des Auswärtigen Amtes, Bonn
   Department II
   Department III
   Department IV
   Department VI
Institut für Internationale Angelegenheiten, Hamburg
Hamburger Weltwirtschafts Archiv
University College Dublin, Archives Department
   Dan Bryan Papers
Caritasverband Archive, Freiburg
Irish Red Cross Archive, Dublin
   Executive Committee Minutes No. 3 1945–50
   Central Council Minutes No. 2 1941–45
   Central Council Minutes No. 3 1945–47
   Central Council Minutes No. 4 1947–48
   Chairman's Reports Meetings 1948–49
Keesings Contemporary Archives

NEWSPAPERS AND JOURNALS

Bulletin of the Department of External Affairs
Cork Examiner
Daily Herald
Der Fortschritt

Der Spiegel
Die Zeit
Diplomatischer Kurier
Enniscorthy Echo
Evening Mail
Frankfurter Allgemeine Zeitung
Irish Independent
Irish Press
Irish Times
Irish Trade Journal
Kölner Rundschau
Limerick Chronicle
Limerick Leader
Rundschau Bonn
The Bulletin
The Standard

INTERVIEWS

Ernest Berkenheier, Wicklow
Helmut und Elisabeth Clissmann, Dublin
Michael Donnellan, Limerick
Seán Egan, Dublin
J. B. Gubbins, Limerick
Peter Kaudewitz, Bad Wimpfen
Rosemary Kavanagh, Dublin
Eberhard Langer, Hamburg
Mr McQuillean, Dublin
Herbert Remmel, Schwerin
Joe Roche, Dublin
Enno Stephan, Varel
Dermot Tittle, Wicklow

UNPUBLISHED SOURCES

Memoirs of W. D. Klüber
Diary of Werner Stephan
Unpublished manuscripts of Heinrich Becker

BIBLIOGRAPHY

Bark, Dennis L. and Gress, David R., *A History of West Germany. From Shadow to Substance 1945–1963*, 2nd ed. 1993 (1st ed. 1989), Blackwell Publishers, Oxford UK and Cambridge USA.

Becker, Heinrich, *Dúchas an Iarthair. Das Erbe des Westens.* Eine Probeauswahl von Dokumentationsbeiträgen aus der Privatsammlung des Herausgebers.

Bielenberg, Christabel, *The Road Ahead*, Bantam Press, London.

Böll, Heinrich, *Irisches Tagebuch*, Deutscher Taschenbuch Verlag, 1996, 1st. ed. 1957.

Carroll, Joseph T., *Ireland in the War Years*, Newton Abbot, New York, 1975.

Carter, Carolle J., The spy who brought his Lunch, in: *Eire-Ireland*, Vol. 10, Minnesota, 1975.

Coogan, Tim Pat, *De Valera. Long Fellow, Long Shadow*, Hutchinson, London, 1993.

Dankspende des deutschen Volkes, *Dankspende des deutschen Volkes* Berlin, 1955.

Dickl, Horst, *Die deutsche Außenpolitik und die irische Frage*, Wiesbaden, 1983.

Duggan, John P., *A History of the Irish Army*, Gill and Macmillan, Dublin, 1989.

——, *Herr Hempel at the German Legation in Dublin, 1937–1945*, PhD Diss., Trinity College, Dublin, 1980.

——, *Neutral Ireland and the Third Reich*, Gill and Macmillan, Dublin, 1985.

Dwyer, T. Ryle, *Guests of the State*, Brandon, Kerry, 1994.

Fisk, Robert, *In Time of War,* Deutsch, London, 1983.

Flamm, Dr Franz, *Die Auslandshilfe für die Stadt Freiburg im Breisgau 1945–1949*, Caritas Archive.

Friedrichs, Werner, *Ein deutsches Denkmal im Stephen's Green*, Schriftenreihe des Deutsch-Irischen Freundeskreises in Baden-Württemberg e.V., Tübingen, 1983.

Gallagher, Frank, *The Indivisible Island*, Gollancz, London, 1957.

Hickmann, Dr Ernst, *Irland. Ein Markt am Rande Europas*, herausg. vom Bremer Ausschuß für Wirtschaftsforschung, Econ-Verlag, Düsseldorf, 1953.

Keatinge, Patrick, *The Formulation of Irish Foreign Policy*, Institute of Public Administration, Dublin, 1973.

Keogh, Dermot, *Twentieth Century Ireland. Nation and State*, Gill and Macmillan, Dublin, 1994. New Gill History of Ireland Bd.5.

Klüber, Wolf Dietrich, *The Naval Engagement Bay of Biscay. Distress and Kerlogue Rescue 28th–29th December 1943*. Unpublished manuscript.

Klüber, Wolf Dietrich, *The Story of the German Navy Personnel Interned in Ireland 1944–1945*. Unpublished manuscript.

Lerchenmüller, J., *Keltischer Sprengstoff*, PhD Diss., Trinity College, Dublin.

Moynihan, M. (Ed.), *Speeches and Statements by Eamon de Valera 1917–1973*, St Martin's Press, New York, 1980.

O'Driscoll, Samuel, *Irish-German Diplomatic Relations 1932–1939*, MA Diss., UCC, 1992.

Sachsen, Ernst Heinrich Prinz von, *Mein Lebensweg vom Königs-schloß zum Bauernhof*, Verl. der Kunst, Dresden, Basel, 1995.

Sagarra, Eda, in: *Im Urteil des Auslandes – Dreißig Jahre Bundes-republik*, C.H. Beck, München, 1979.

Schneider, Jürgen, Sotscheck, Rolf, *Irland. Eine Bibliographie selb-ständiger deutschsprachiger Publikationen 16. Jahrhundert bis 1989*. Verlag der Georg-Büchner Buchhandlung, Darmstadt, 1988.

Smyllie, R.M., Unneutral Neutral Eire, in *Foreign Affairs* No. 24, 1945–1946, S.317–326.

Stephan, Enno, *William Thomas Mulvany (1806–1885). Ein irischer Pionier des Ruhrgebiets*, herausg. von dem deutsch-irischen Freundeskreis in Baden-Württemberg e.V., 1985.

Stephan, Enno, *Spies in Ireland*, Macdonald & Co., London, 1963 (1st ed. Hamburg 1961)

Sturm, Herbert, *Hakenkreuz und Kleeblatt: Irland, die Alliierten und das 'Dritte Reich' 1933–1945*. Frankfurt a. M., Bern, New York, 1984, 2 Bd.

Williams, T.D., *Irish Foreign Policy, 1949–1969*, in: J. J. Lee, *Ireland 1945–1970*, Dublin, 1979. [Publisher to come]

Wollasch, Hans-Josef, *Humanitäre Auslandshilfe für Deutschland nach dem zweiten Weltkrieg* ed. by Deutscher caritasverband, Freiburg in Bresgau, 1976.

Index

133